PRETTY GIRL

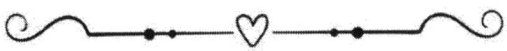

WITH

THE WALKER

TEARS OF A WARRIOR PT. 2

BY: AVIANCE THOMPSON

Copyright © 2024 by Seazons Collections Publishing House.
Copyright © 2024 by Scirocca Publication.
Copyright © 2024 by Aviance Thompson.

All rights reserved. No part of this book may be reproduced or used in any manner without written permission of the copyright owner.

My Acknowledgments

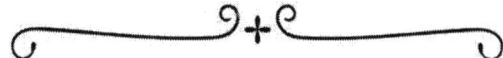

I honor myself for choosing life, even when it felt overwhelming and uncertain. I recognize the immense courage it has taken to face my fears, to stand in the face of adversity, and to resist the temptation of the easier path. I celebrate my bravery in embracing the unknown, stepping into risks, and persisting despite the emotional storms that have tested me in ways I never imagined. This journey has been one of the most profoundly challenging experiences of my life, demanding strength I didn't always know I had.

These tears are not of defeat but of resilience—the tears of a warrior who has fought battles within and emerged stronger, wiser, and more determined. Today, I reclaim this moment for myself as an act of self-love, self-respect, and deep gratitude for the journey I've endured. This time, it's about me, for me; this time, this is for myself!

Acknowledging Dr. Dreszer

Dr. Dreszer,

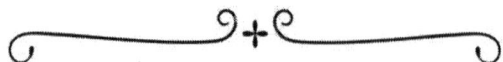

Your unwavering love and tireless dedication in the face of this extraordinary circumstance will remain etched in my heart forever. From the very beginning, you pledged to give your all to my journey, and you delivered that promise with every ounce of your being. You will never fade from my memory; you have become an inseparable part of who I am. The passion and care you pour into your calling now flow through me, a testament to your impact. Though the path has been anything but easy, you instilled in me the hope and belief that finding a reason to smile again was not only possible but inevitable.

Thank you to you and all of the Vanguard staff.

TABLE OF CONTENTS

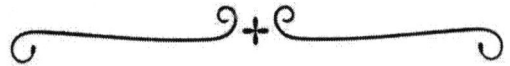

My Acknowledgments		iii
Acknowledging Dr. Dreszer		iv
Chapter One:	Revelation	1
Chapter Two:	Unsettled Nostalgia	8
Chapter Three:	Progressing Is Depressing	21
Chapter Four:	Post Op	27
Chapter Five:	Tied By Blood And Emotions	31
Chapter Six:	Its Complicated	47
Chapter Seven:	The Importance Of A Father	55
Chapter Eight:	Beneath The Bandages	71
Chapter Nine:	Healing Waves	85
Chapter Ten:	Issues Of The Heart	94
Chapter Eleven:	Evaluation	105
Chapter Twelve:	Shadow Work	120
Chapter Thirteen:	Discomposed Reality	134
Chapter Fourteen:	Survivors Complex	137

CHAPTER ONE

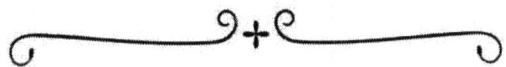

REVELATION

I wailed while walking into physical therapy. Three years later, and I couldn't believe I was still going through this shit! I stood at the front desk, patiently awaiting assistance. Approaching me came a short, dark-haired woman. "You must be Majic!" she said excitedly.

"Yes," I responded.

"Have a seat; someone will be with you shortly," she replied.

I took a seat, shaking my right leg in nervousness. This time was different. It was real different. One definite way I was able to put this situation behind me was by concealing the damage it caused. I kept my thigh wrapped so that it wouldn't constantly remind me of a time I tried my best to forget. A time that broke me into tiny bits and pieces, that still seemed impossible to put back together. My thigh was mangled, unrecognizable, as if it had been mauled. And there was absolutely nothing I could do about it. It was burdensome to look at, as I struggled to get out of bed some days. I decided that I was going to wrap it, and it became a permanent coping mechanism. On top of that, if I didn't, none of my clothes would fit properly. The circumference comparison to my other leg was a major difference, and the look of the bare wound would scare people nearly half to death. It was that bad!

"Majic Daniels." A tall guy with a head full of grey hair called my name. It was time to go to the back. As I followed him to be examined, tears began to fill my eyes again. I was overly emotional because I knew what was coming next. As he assessed my leg, it was hard as fuck seeing and hearing his reaction. They never wanted to offend me, but I knew what it was. After the examination, he concluded that it was only bending 20 degrees. That was damn near nothing. He explained that when I came back for my next session, it would be necessary for me to leave the bandage off. Before he could finish his sentence, my cries filled the room. It had now been two whole years since I'd seen what my thigh looked like. When it was time to clean it, I reached inside with a hot, soapy washcloth. When it needed fixing, I added gauze and rearranged it all without fully taking it off. The times I unwrapped it, I did it all while never looking down. I just felt my way through. Mentally, it terrified me. But it was now time to face it. I wept the whole way home, up until the following appointment.

I sat in my car and cried every day after dropping the girls off at school. Sometimes I'd go to Crystal's house and sadly sit there while she encouraged me as much as she could.

Time crept up on me so fast; before I knew it, it was Wednesday. I was due to go back in the morning, so it was time to take the dressing off.

I called my daddy, sobbing so much I could barely breathe or talk. Mari had just finished cutting through all of the gauze, and from what I saw, I was surprised I was still able to stand. It was as if she had just removed my whole entire thigh. There was nothing there. My hip and thigh literally looked like a stick. As I looked down, I immediately weakened. My anxiety flared, and I began to hyperventilate. My daddy said he was on his way, but I told him it was okay because I was too ashamed. Mari suggested that we call the ambulance because of my anxiety attack, but I hated having to explain what happened to me. It was so complex, and the people who didn't know assumed it was something that happened as recently as last night because I'd been dealing with it for so long.

When it came to the way my leg looked, I hid it from the girls as well. I just wanted them to live as if this shit never happened. But no matter how hard I tried, it was impossible. This was my life now. Mari seemed pretty strong about it. She often wanted to do something that pertained to helping me with dressing and undressing it. I wasn't sure if she was strong, numb, or just wanted to be an assistance to me.

As Mari grew older, she started to become a bit cold in demeanor. She was nonchalant and hardly ever expressed herself. I mostly had to force it out of her.

On the other hand, I never let Zuri see anything pertaining to it. She was hyperactive, but she wore her heart on her sleeve. She was extremely sensitive and expressed her love to me every chance she got. She'd draw pictures or write letters; it didn't matter, but I was always going to know how much she appreciated her mommy. I loved that she was that way because I wanted them to enjoy being children and to act as if they had never been hurt. Even though that's what I desired, a part of their innocence was gone when it came to that. The accident had now exposed them to what pain truly felt like. Prior to that, that wasn't something they really experienced. When I left Steve, Mari felt the effect the most, but I worked overtime to make sure she was happy and thriving. I had to because I wore their emotions as if they were my own. If I didn't make sure they were doing okay emotionally, I'd be suffering as well.

I pulled into physical therapy, exited the car, and headed for the building. My eyes were bloodshot red walking inside. I was restless and falling apart. I hoped they didn't think I was under any kind of influence. But quite possibly, I was. There was no influence greater than pain. Pain had the ability to turn you into an addict or the best version of yourself. As soon as I signed in, the therapist called me to the back to get undressed. He eyeballed my leg in silence and couldn't believe what he saw. "WOW, you're very blessed to still be with us. And they were able to save it as well!" he said in disbelief.

And he was right. The firefighters, doctors, and surgeons worked tirelessly. I'm still amazed as I watched them consistently exhaust all options when it came to my well-being. Being trapped under the dashboard, I knew there wasn't much hope. But their persistence had a lot to do with me being alive today. Kiara said I flatlined twice that morning, once before the surgery and during the procedure.

The therapist told me he didn't think there was much that could be done for it to bend, but he at least wanted to get it to bend to 35 degrees. "Now that your leg is undressed, you should go to the plastic surgeon to start your reconstruction process." The reconstructive surgery was mentioned in the past, but I never quite prepared myself to go back. Truth be told, it was time. I became stagnant in the space I was in, all out of fear. I told myself that day, "It's unwrapped now; it can only get better from here." I picked up the phone and called the surgeon. He remembered me and asked that I come in right away. I felt like I was losing my mind. I didn't know how to feel. It was happening all too fast.

In that moment, I experienced all sorts of emotions. And on top of it, I was alone. I got in my car and began to drive. Tears filled my eyes, streaming down my cheeks.

I could hear Rod Wave faintly playing in the background. "I know God gives his toughest battles to his strongest soldiers; don't cry for me when the war is over." Then he went on to say, "Living life on the run, too many problems at once, too stressed, can't get no rest, I'm up before the sun. I knew this day would come; even though it's hard times, it's too late to give up now, my nigga, you gotta keep it moving on."

And he was right. It wasn't a coincidence I was hearing this song. Everything in life happens how it is supposed to. This was divine timing. The Most High knew what I needed and when I needed it. In that moment, those words had given me so much life. I sat up in my seat, put my hand on top of the steering wheel with my right elbow on the console, and started whipping that shit! I turned on Boosie because he was able to adjust my mood in any feeling of defeat. I walked into the doctor's office feeling much better than what I had been experiencing the last few days.

They all knew my situation and were excited to see me. Walking in, they were giving me many compliments and acknowledging how far I'd come. "It's nice to see you, Majic. What took you so long?" asked Dr. Jessie.

This shit was still all really deep for me. But he totally understood. He instructed me to change into the gown, and they would be back in shortly.

He, another surgeon, and his assistant walked in together,

closing the door behind them. I became anxious all over again. I began getting hot while heat protruded its way out of my mouth. Dr. Jessie told me to stand and open my gown. After following his order, his facial expression spoke before any words would form from his mouth. "Wow, it's fully disfigured!" He couldn't believe his eyes. He ran out of the room to get more staff. Their reaction wasn't as bad as his, but I think they just didn't want to offend me. I knew the state of my leg, so I didn't expect anything less. Anyone would have reacted that way.

They eyed me carefully, examining my whole body with a fine-tooth comb, trying to figure out where they would take from and exactly how. I almost had one hundred percent muscle and nerve damage to my thigh, so they were looking for more than just fat. They decided to take the vertical recuts from the left side of my abdomen and apply them to the left side of my thigh to complete a flap. It could only be done with muscle that still had the blood vessels attached. They wanted to try to restore some of the muscle damage for functional purposes and the soft tissue for fullness. He told me it was only the beginning for many surgeries to come because it was impossible to fix all that needed to be fixed in one day. "This is a difficult situation, very tedious. There's a lot to be done here, but I'm ready when you are!" He asked when I wanted to start. I responded, "ASAP!" It was currently the month of May; we scheduled for July because he was already booked. I started to get dressed and was able to let out a sigh of relief. Lately, I'd been under an extreme amount of stress. But on the bright side, I faced one of my biggest challenges, and I'm so proud of me. I don't give myself enough credit because I always want more. But that was a major step forward for me. Anytime someone mentioned me going to the orthopedic, I'd change the subject, all because I had to remove my dressing. I lived with this in my mind every day. I knew it had to be done, but it hurt me deeply. I was excited and nervous all at the same time, but I couldn't wait to see what they could do. Anything was better than its current state.

CHAPTER TWO

UNSETTLED NOSTALGIA

Sitting there, fidgeting with my fingers and talking to my sister, thoughts of Nick took over. We still weren't on speaking terms, but I sure did need him right now. He and Krystal conversed often; she suggested that with my surgery being as serious as it was, it would be a great idea for me to reach out and fill him in. She was right. The fact that they were relocating and reattaching vessels was kind of scary. I wanted to mend things between us anyway because our fallouts were never that serious. They were mainly because he took a lot of things I said out of context. He was so quick to get offended, and his fight response was to shut down. He chose to walk away every time rather than talk about what went wrong and how it made him feel. When he was mad, I just had to let him get over it because nothing I said was going to get through to him. So, by my sister telling me to reach out, it wasn't happening—mainly because I didn't want to be rejected. That was a wound I struggled with but was attempting to heal. He ignored my last attempts, so I left it in my sister's hands.

    I drifted into a daze, thinking of me going into cardiac arrest again, and it scared the shit out of me. Thinking about the chance of something going wrong and him not knowing made me feel a way. I felt like it was due to him. He held a special place in my heart. That was some shit I couldn't shake, no matter how hard I tried. I knew he loved me as well, but he was always able to convince me otherwise by the way he was able to disconnect.

    It was the day before surgery, and I had been awaiting it with endless anticipation. I had quite a bit of relief—not excited, but more so ready to get it over with. I despised surgery, but I knew I needed to begin the process.

    I told the girls to get their belongings situated and prepare to go with Kim for the weekend. "Mommy, we're ready!" they said. They were all packed and ready to go. As I pulled into Kim's house, we exited the car to hug one another.

    "I love y'all," I said.

    "We love you too, Mommy," they replied. "Goodnight, we're going to pray for you." One thing I taught them was to always pray, whether things are going right or wrong. Don't be scared to ask God for direction and give thanks. I sat there and watched them until they walked into the house before I pulled off. Tears began to flow. I loved those girls with all my heart, and just thinking about how they would react if I didn't make it back to them was something I couldn't fathom. I was living for them, so I had to make it back; there was no other option.

    I walked in the house and double-checked my bag. There was a book to keep me occupied, comfortable clothing for after surgery, a toothbrush, a scarf, my charger, and some snacks. I laid down to try and get some rest, but I was restless. I lay awake all night praying for my safety. I cried some, but I worshiped more. No matter how it may seem, I knew that I was blessed beyond measure. It was natural to worry when you were going through something, but I knew above all that I was covered. I knew the Most High, and I knew I was a chosen one. My work here wasn't quite done yet.

I awoke at 4 a.m. to my alarm going off. I made my bed, undressed out of my nightgown, and showered with antibacterial soap as instructed—all while never once looking down. I had a hard time understanding how I was still even able to stand. It was all just surreal to me. But my strength was more questionable because I got up every day and did it.

It was required that I check in to the hospital at 5:30 a.m. because surgery was at 7 a.m. I was their first case. I left my house at 4:45. I went to pick up my sister; she was dropping me off. The whole ride there, I remember my stomach being in knots. My emotions were all over the place. I didn't have expectations of what I wanted things to look like, but I wanted to feel that it was all worth it. I wanted to be in a better situation than I currently was, but each time I was examined, they always reminded me how lucky I was to even be alive. So I was just grateful. I didn't dwell on the physical aspects too much because I was fine as fuck regardless.

We finally arrived at the hospital after what felt like hours. My daddy was there waiting when I walked in. "Hey, how about you? You okay? You ain't got nothing to worry about. Just leave everything in His hands; God got you." Every day leading up to the surgery, he called me with encouraging words. No matter what he did, he never forgot the word of God.

They called my number, and we headed to the back. "Hi, Ms.

Daniels, how are you?" a beautiful nurse with long black hair and a caramel complexion asked.

"I'm fine," I responded. But she clearly saw that I wasn't. My tone wasn't matching up to what I was saying. Soon after, I started to get agitated. My anxiety kicked in, and I began to think of Nick; he was my comfort zone. Krystal told him about the surgery a little over a month ago, and he responded in a concerned manner, asking that she keep him updated. Exactly a month prior to today, he texted her to see how surgery was going, but he mistakenly mixed June up with July.

It was refreshing to know that he cared and that it was on his mind just as much as it was on mine. He reached out to express his concern, so we were back in touch. But because our fallout was kind of bad last time, I wasn't comfortable being too personal. I didn't want to do too much. Even though it was in my heart, he said some things that made me feel a way. But his actions always contradicted his words. His mouth would say the opposite of what his actions were showing. And they always showed he was physically and emotionally invested, but he wouldn't allow his words to express it.

But still, a conversation with him right now was what I needed. It would have lightened my mood. I thought about calling the girls, but all they were going to do was make me more anxious. Mari worried for me a lot. They often asked if I was going to be okay and if I would be back home tomorrow. Our conversations got the best of me. They were my weakness. They were the only way to break me down. Our pre-surgery conversations mostly resulted in us crying, and that's something I didn't need right now.

There were four nurses surrounding me, and with all of them doing different things to me, I grew extremely uneasy. My breathing became heavy, and before I knew it, I was telling them to get the fuck off me! I was hyperventilating and mimicking signs of an anxiety attack. They became more frequent after the accident. It was somewhat the new norm for me. It was like I could take on the world physically, but mentally I couldn't take much of anything. I looked over at Krystal as she cried, reacting to my reaction. Trying to mask it, she stepped out of the room.

Nick: "Can I call?"

Nick: "If not, I want to say I pray for you, soooo I know that you will pull through with amazing results. You are already great as you are. I love you, girl! I will talk to you in a few once you come out."

It was time for me to turn my belongings over; there wasn't any time left for me to respond. The anesthesiologist injected me with Versed and began to push me down the hallway towards the operating room. My cries turned into moans, and my moans turned into silence as the weight of the world sat comfortably on my eyelids. We made it to our destination. My X-rays crowded the room. There were many surgical instruments and a bunch of other scary stuff, but my body was too limp to react. The anesthesiologist put a plastic mask over my face, covering my nose and mouth. "Ms. Daniels, I need you to take heavy breaths in and out." I inhaled and exhaled until I was no longer a part of existence.

"Majic, Majic!" Doctor Jessie called my name, shaking me profusely. "You did wonderful; everything went as planned. How are you feeling?" The pain was excruciating. I instantly burst into tears. They injected me with something to take away the pain, putting me to sleep immediately.

When I woke up, it was dark out. Fifteen missed calls, twenty-one messages, and countless notifications from social media. Most times, I'd take a picture before going into surgery. There were people I didn't know personally who were on this journey with me. They'd send encouraging words and motivational messages. They didn't even know they were helping me just as much as I was helping them. I recovered a little, enough to return some calls and respond to messages.

Me: "I'm out."

Nick: "I told you that you had nothing to worry about, girl. God got you."

And he was right. I was special. I went on social media to let everyone know I was okay. "I'm out, y'all boyyyzzzz! Gone head and salute a real girl!" Because at this point, I was undefeated!

I returned Mari and Zuri's call. "Mommy, we been calling you. You okay? We were scared."

"Didn't I tell y'all I'm always coming back for y'all?"

They started to tell me about their day, but I kept dozing off from all the medication. I talked to them for a little while longer until I could no longer fight it. I told them to get ready for bed; I'll talk to them tomorrow. That medicine had me high as fuck. The easy part was over, but the hardest part had just begun.

Mentally, physically, and emotionally, surgery always took a major toll on me. But the mental part was something I could never get a hold of. It whooped my ass every time.

"Ms. Daniels, it's time to take your blood pressure and empty your drains," a nurse says while entering the room and turning on the lights. I was asleep most of the day; I didn't get to see the result of the surgery. When I looked down, my leg was wrapped, but it appeared to be fuller. There was a large amount of padding also, and I know that played a role in its current state. My stomach was bandaged also.

Going through this pain alone was normally the start of my depression. I sat up in the bed as much as I could, straining to get my right leg off the bed. I felt it in my stomach. I began to slide my left leg a Little at a time until it was at the edge of the bed, I eased it onto the floor. I initiated to stand but felt lightheaded immediately. "Sit down, Ms. Daniels, until I can assist you." I continued to stand while closing my eyes until I felt it was okay to open them. I put my right foot first, dragging my left leg to meet it as I took a step. I knew it was too soon, but I had to do what I needed to stay positive. I knew myself, and once I was in a place physically where I couldn't do much, depression was right around the corner. This was very important for my mental health; I had to keep moving forward.

For me to have multiple diagnosed mental illnesses, it was a necessity for me to take care of my mind. I made it my job because as soon as I neglected it, I drowned. Because of my issues, it was easy to get sidetracked. Depression has been trying to take me out since I was a child. I continued to step forward, making it to the bathroom with the assistance of my walker.

I washed up after using the restroom. While walking back to my bed, I saw my phone lighting up. Slowly putting one foot before the other, my phone lit up again. As I made it to the edge of the bed, I slowly eased down, holding my breath. The pain coming from my midsection barely allowed me to breathe properly. As I sat down to catch my breath, I reached for my phone, and it was going off again.

Different people were sending videos of Jason proposing to his baby mama. As I watched him get on one knee, my skin started to burn, and heat forced its way out of my mouth again. I couldn't believe that fuck nigga! My emotions weren't coming from wanting to be with him; I had not an ounce of feeling for him intimately.

I maneuvered daily as if he was never a part of my life. The way I felt about him was almost as if he never existed. My emotions came from it now being three years since the accident, and I'm still in this situation. I'm still having surgeries; I couldn't get on my knee and propose to a nigga, even if I was stupid enough to. My life was now different. But he was still living a normal life—a regular life—because his wasn't altered. He was still able to carry on daily without interference. The way I physically interacted with my girls changed forever. I can't run behind them. My leg and foot painfully swell after only a short amount of time being on them. There are things they want to do and places they want to go, and as their mother, it's required of me, but many times I'm not able. But regardless, I make it happen and just suffer in silence.

Surgery after surgery, I'm in the hospital by my motherfucking self. And for a woman to know he put me in this situation and didn't hold him accountable for his actions, I see exactly why it was so easy for him to abandon me. After something so serious, she was still able to welcome him back with open arms. In all honesty, she was just as weak as he was. I wasn't his side bitch; from my understanding, he wanted to build something. He was on my ass about being his ol' lady. He supposedly hadn't been with her and was never going back. I didn't hate him because that's too much power to give him. But the man I thought he was became clear to me that he wasn't. I saw him after Rico confronted him. "You're so beautiful, Maj; I think about you every day that passes by." But never once could he look me in my eyes. I learned a long time ago that was the trait of a snake. And to be honest, I didn't want him to. I just wanted him to do what he did best, and that was to leave and act like he never knew me. I didn't want anything to do with him. He was a liar and manipulative.

My growth made me realize that nigga didn't even deserve to smile in a real bitch's face. Being understanding was the least of my concerns now. I'd sit and think about the times we were together and came to the realization that if I really paid attention, I would've seen inconsistencies in some of the things he said. But I wasn't tripping on him. The vibes were good. For once, it wasn't me doing all the outpouring. It had been a while since someone filled my cup in return, and that was his energy consistently.

Being that we were still dating and hadn't made it official, I played a lot of things cool. The few times his situation became a topic, he reassured me that he moved on before I came into his life. The way he adored me and thought I was the most beautiful girl in the world wasn't a reason for me to think he was being dishonest. He even lied to his baby mama about the accident.

The morning the incident occurred, Kiara called Keyshia to explain what took place. "Maj was in an accident; the boy fell asleep at the wheel, and she's not going to make it! And we can't find him!" Keyshia didn't take it well. She began screaming and crying on the phone, "I told Maj I didn't trust that bitch!" Keyshia cried. She never liked Jason. She never formally met him and wasn't interested in it. She wasn't fond of him since the time I had to tell him to go to the hospital when his baby mama was in labor.

After Kiara and Keyshia hung up, Keyshia went on my Facebook to find the baby mama. She searched my page until she found Jason's name and found her from his page.

Keyshia instantly sent her a message:

"Call me ASAP!" The girl immediately opened it.

Keyshia: "Majic is in a coma. Jason was driving my friend, and now she's in a coma!"

Baby mama: "What?! Who is Majic?"

Keyshia: "Jason and my best friend were dating. Him, her, and her daughters were on the way to Georgia to see her family, and he fell asleep at the wheel."

Baby mama: "Omg, WHAT????? Jason lied! He said he was on the road with his friends, and a girl who was with one of his homeboys was hurt a little, but she was going to be okay."

Keyshia: "That bitch is lying! My friend is about to fuckin die!"

Baby mama: "Omg, I can't believe him!"

Keyshia: "Him and my friend have been talking, and he used to be at my house every day."

Baby mama: "We've been having problems, but that's normal for us. It wasn't ever anything like we weren't getting back together; that's what we always do. But I figured he was seeing someone else. I could tell. He was acting different."

Keyshia: "Gurl, that bitch is going to jail!"

Baby mama: *sits down to catch her breath* "Omg, I'm on my way to the doctor now to get my stitches taken out from my C-section, and he's not even here. But I have to go; we will talk soon."

I've been awake all night, in my head. I was a blessing to many. I gave the world hope. But it was rarely anyone I could call when I needed a listening ear because I was the one with all the answers. I kind of preferred to deal with things alone anyway because I didn't maneuver similarly to the average person. I'm an extremely logical thinker, and I was responding from the 5th dimension. Most didn't understand why I reacted the way I did. Many people around me were still operating from a 3D consciousness. They were looking at things from a purely physical state. "Things were perceived as good or bad, and life was a competition." Fulfillment was found in making money and social status. There was no desire to go within or to look at things from a deeper standpoint. Life was played out by skimming the surface. There wasn't a desire to dig deep or to understand the deeper meaning behind things and what was really transpiring. In 5D, there was a higher purpose for all things, and every experience held meaning. There were stronger feelings for love and connection. Love and compassion reigned supreme, and there was a lack of judgment. I understood that everyone was just on their own journey. From this state, competition didn't exist. There was a desire to just live from a place of pure authenticity. My purpose was just to live in my truth and seek joy.

So usually, I wanted to be alone. Spiritual maintenance was the best way to make me feel better. I'd cleanse my space, fast, pray, and as a result, I was left feeling renewed. I was a peaceful person; I just believed in letting the Most High do His work.

I looked down as my phone rang; it was Keyshia. Hell, before I could finish my sentence, Keyshia was on the other end screaming!

"Gurl, fuck that nigga and that ugly-ass hoe; she couldn't sit with you on your worst day." I chuckled a little. She had a way of making me feel better because our conversations made me feel like the circumstances were different. Everything just felt different every time we talked. She had the ability to make me feel like none of this ever happened. She continued talking, "We should've let his light bulb head ass get dealt with when everybody was looking for him." One thing about my girl: she was gonna tell it like it is, and she wasn't ashamed. I was exactly one month older than she was, but she tried to protect me in every way possible. We were the same in a lot of ways, but we were different in many also. I was soft and feminine. She dressed like a girl, but her masculinity outweighed her femininity. I had this innocence about me she felt like she needed to protect. She always tried to put me down with the good guys, the quiet ones. She knew I only wanted to be loved, so she seemed scared for me. She felt people would take advantage.

And she was right. I was attracted to the way a man thought. Mindset turned me on real bad. I didn't care about the materials. Of course, you needed the basic necessities, and I loved a well-groomed man—one who could dress and was respectful. But being focused on what they could do for me and how much money they had was never my concern. Plus, I was scared to depend on a man, especially financially. Hyper-independent was best to describe me now. I was afraid—actually terrified—at the thought of depending on someone. That's not how I wanted to be, but I couldn't help it. It was a result of trauma, now a coping mechanism. Oftentimes, those who had some sort of abandonment issues or parents who were absent, inconsistent, or unable to meet their emotional needs grew up believing people weren't reliable. I was afraid of depending on someone to do something or holding onto their word and then they let me down. So that became a dealbreaker for me. I took that the most seriously in any relationship I involved myself in. If a man couldn't keep his word, it wasn't nothing else for us to discuss. Even though it may not have had anything to do with me, I took that to heart. It had a way of making me feel unworthy. That's why a man who didn't possess the characteristic of leadership didn't interest me.

But just because I didn't ask for nothing, it didn't mean I didn't require anything. I feel like when a man is in the presence of a good woman, he is supposed to treat her as such. And since I never asked, that made me deserving of everything. If I felt like I was in the presence of a great man, he would never have to open his mouth for anything. So it was also important for me to be with a giver. I loved gift-giving. If I fucked with you like that, I was definitely showering you and showing my appreciation. Because God didn't make a lot of real niggas.

CHAPTER THREE

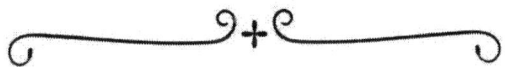

PROGRESSING IS DEPRESSING

Four days passed, and I'm aggravated as fuck, ready to go home! Being in the hospital did something to my spirit in a major way. It sparked up emotions from a time when I was at my lowest. I literally lost my mind when the accident occurred. No words will ever be great enough to describe what I felt. The amount of tears I shed could have flooded the Pacific Ocean. The anger I felt could have started a forest fire. I was defeated, with no more fight left in me, but I was relentless. My soul wouldn't give up, no matter how badly my flesh wanted to. There were days I awoke and was mad that I was still living. Everybody would tell me, "Maj, you gotta fight; you can't give up." But they didn't understand. It was easier said than done. Every time the doctors came into my room, it was bad news after bad news after motherfucking bad news. What the fuck was I fighting for? But when I thought about it, I was always reminded of my girls; that's what I was fighting for. They were my only reason why. They always brought me back to being optimistic.

In my current physical condition, I've come a long way from that moment. But being in the same environment, constantly being cut on, not being able to walk afterward, and having to stay, did a number on me. Usually, I'd start taking extra care of my mind and eating right before my scheduled surgeries so things wouldn't feel so familiar, and I wouldn't find myself in the same place, but nothing helped once I was back in that same setting.

"Knock, knock…"
"Come in!"
My dad: "Wassup?"
Me: "Hey, what's up, da?"
My dad: "How you feeling?"
Me: "I'm getting depressed; I'm ready to go," I cried.
My daddy: "It's okay; the hard part is over."
But in reality, it wasn't….

I slowly opened the food he brought for me to eat. I mainly ate salads at the hospital, but I was tired of that shit. I knew I had to be down about five pounds. I was hungry and needed to eat but didn't have much of an appetite. I was starving in ways that didn't require nutrients. I forced myself to eat a couple of bites before closing it. I told him I was exhausted and needed rest. He gave me a hug and told me not to hesitate to call if I needed him. My dad and I's relationship was going steady. He was calling to check up on me almost every day leading up to my surgery. After surgery as well. We were trying to get it together, but I knew it was only a matter of time before we bumped heads again. We were so much alike. He would always tell his friends, "Boy, she ain't shit to be played with." And he was right, but it was deeper than that. There were so many things that needed to be addressed between us. Every time we fell out, it was me who initiated reconciliation. I didn't understand that. If you love me so much, why can't you ever be the adult and come to me as my father? He never showed emotion. He acted as if he had to be tough in every situation. As a man, I understood that because I would tell Nick the same thing. He didn't have to be so tough all the time; he responded, "I have to be that way for me and you." But I felt like when it came to your daughters or the women in your life, that should be the only place where it was okay for you to be emotionally exposed. Everyone actually has duality, and feminine energy isn't limited to just females. It's called emotional balance. It actually proves they are secure in their masculinity. I can't remember one time my daddy has ever consoled me. He did when I was in ICU, but that was because I was dying. And that's the only time people feel it's okay to show love, but that's when it's far too late. I can tell there was a substantial amount of things he wanted to say, but he never actually delivered them. It was as if his pride wouldn't allow him to release the words. Our relationship was like we were homies. We joked around a lot; I mean, we laughed until we couldn't breathe. He told me he loved me a lot as well, but it was more so after something happened. As in, "You know I love you, right?" But I didn't understand why it took that. I was his only daughter, only child to be exact. It hurt to know that not even my dad could love me properly. Although I've learned a lot, I still don't exactly know what true love feels like. To a girl, a father is her first love.

    It's true, my granddaddy was everything and more, but he wore many hats. He was busy. He ran a business; he was a husband, father, and grandfather. He was spread so thin but still managed to care for everyone. He gave us his all. He was old but still went to work every day in the hot sun. By the time he made it home, there wasn't much of him left to give. But the greatest love

I've ever received came from him. He tried. He never made excuses. He gave one hundred percent in everything he did. He was consistent. That's what a man was. That's who I admired, and that's who I want my husband to be an example of.

It was important for children to have healthy emotional relationships. They needed that emotional support and stability to feel happy and safe. Emotional neglect resulted in depression, low self-esteem, and a whole bunch of other shit that would leave a long-term effect. It would change their outlook on love, how they express themselves, and their ability to set healthy boundaries. As I look back, there were so many things I settled for out of fear, thinking I wouldn't find better. Not knowing what I deserved, I sat There was an uncomfortable space. Hoping things would get better, when in reality, it would only get worse because I was teaching them how to treat me.

So, because of my dad's absence and lack of support, it seemed as if he lost all rights to me. When he visited my grandparents' home, my granddaddy made it clear he couldn't discipline us. One day in particular, I arrived home after school, and my dad was there. My granddaddy hired him to come over and paint. While I was on the phone conversing with a friend, he told me to hang up. There was something he asked me to do; I responded, "Okay, I'm coming." But it seemed as if he had a deeper issue with me that day. He continued to give me funny looks, sizing me up. I assumed that maybe he didn't like the shorts I wore to school and felt some type of way about that. I'm not really sure.

Destiny and I were talking amongst one another like, "What the fuck is wrong with him?" But one thing for sure, my grandparents didn't play with us about the things we wore. If my grandma didn't see a problem with it, there was no problem. Every morning, she was up like a sergeant, making sure we were appropriately dressed, especially me. I stuck out; I was the fashionista, and I loved showing skin. Big thighs ran in our family. And if I got the chance, I was showing what my mama gave me. Before I could hang up the phone, he grabbed me by my shirt, pulling me towards my room. He took off his belt and started hitting me, asking why I was acting that way. I seriously didn't know what it was he was speaking of because I wasn't doing anything inappropriate. I wouldn't cry, so the hits became harder. My daddy was about six foot, two hundred and something pounds, solid. He was big—not fat, muscle-bound. He continued to hit me until I bruised and swelled up. Big thick marks covered my arms and legs. He tried to talk to me afterward, but I wouldn't respond. Tears just fell from my face. I couldn't believe he put his hands on me.

"My granddaddy hired him for a job, not to come play daddy," that's what I was thinking. Because that's just what he was doing—"playing daddy." I left my room and called my granddaddy. As soon as I heard his voice, I burst into tears. I looked out the window, awaiting his arrival. I saw his white Lincoln flying down the street. He jumped out of the car while it was almost still in drive. He was walking so fast trying to get in the house that he was twisting.

"Jim, I know goddamn well you ain't put your hands on my motherfucking daughter! You ain't have no goddamn business touching my motherfucking kids! These are my goddamn kids; I take care of them! And I know motherfucking well you ain't touch her! Now I want your big red ass to still be standing there when I get back, and I'm gonna show you better than I can tell you!" he yelled.

My granddaddy didn't take bullshit from anyone! My grandma was scared for me to go to school the next day because of the bruises. And because they were my guardians, they were responsible. When I went to school, I wanted to tell on his ass so bad, but I knew I couldn't without it falling on my grandparents. I had a counselor since 7th grade, and she followed me all the way to high school. She was now a family friend, and my grandma loved her. She came to see me at school, and she wasn't happy. She reminded me that she was supposed to report things like that, but in my case, she didn't, for the sake of my grandmother.

CHAPTER FOUR

POST OP

It was now time for discharge. In my home, where it was only me, I wasn't much help to myself, let alone my girls. But since I really didn't have a choice, it was time to put on my big girl panties. I didn't have time to lay there and heal. Mari and Zuri had to eat. So whether I was cooking or going out to buy something, whatever I decided, I still needed my legs. I usually walked Zuri to school because it was near our home. I couldn't just sit there; things still had to be taken care of, and I wasn't going to allow them to lack because of what I was going through. Sometimes I called Uncle Deon and Krystal, but I didn't like to bother people too much with my problems, and it was also hard for me to say that I was in need. But if I called my Uncle Deon, he was coming. No matter what I needed, what I wanted, or how far I was, you just better pray like hell it wasn't you I was calling him for. He was quiet as a mouse but as dangerous as a lion. His love for me and my girls never wavered. That was my heart. He was like that with

Krystal and Kiara also. He was everything to us, all in one.

No matter how I dressed it up, it was a battle. No one ever knew what I was going through because I isolated myself and resurfaced when I was stronger. I confided in Nick a lot, but I had my limits with him also because I didn't want him to feel I was weak and needy. But the times I felt desolate, he was the only one that could turn it around in that moment. And as much as I loved my girls, they couldn't give me the comfort that he did. It was the level of protection he provided me. It was the feeling of being cared for and considered. He made it okay for me to sit my load down a while and be completely vulnerable. It was the excitement of love that kept you going when you're going through a life-changing situation. Of course, your children are your reason to live, but when someone is there loving you through the pain, reassuring you that everything is going to be okay, sticking by your side no matter what the outcome may look like—no matter how messed up you may be, they choose to stick by you. That's what it felt like for me. I could've been completely defenseless around him and wouldn't have panicked because it was evident he would have never allowed anything to happen to me.

Getting out of the car, ambulating was now even worse. It had been a while since I'd had surgery. The last one was my colostomy reversal two years ago. There were daily struggles, but they weren't as difficult as this. This shit had me down. I had three drains: one coming from the side of my thigh and two from the bottom of my stomach. Watching blood slowly drain from my body, emptying them as they refilled, and making sure the drainage remained the right color kept me anxious. It was all so stressful. I was trying my best to stay positive, but I couldn't shake that shit. I constantly cried because I was in such an awful state of mind. I texted Ericka:

"I can't do this. I'm so tired. I'm just ready to give up." I wanted it all to be over. I put my phone down because I didn't want advice. I expressed the way I was feeling, and I didn't want to make it a debate. I just needed to feel it. Neither did I want sympathy. Someone treating me like I was weak was the fastest way for me to get my act together. And I had my mind made up: I wanted to die! But I could never bring myself to cause self-affliction, even though I was in distress. I lay in my bed suffering painful emotions, cried until my pillow was drenched with sorrow. Ericka didn't care that I wasn't answering; she popped right up! Even though I didn't want to talk, and neither did I want company, I appreciated her concern. We shared emotions and even cried together. I felt better. She left soon after; there was work she needed to complete. The lingering effect I was left with was rejuvenating. I turned on my music; the equanimity was remarkable when I was facing a meltdown.

It was sure indeed my physical state sustained the most to the naked eye, but by far, my mental state took the greatest hit! "Get my mommy out of the car!" are words that I will never forget. They haunt me to this day. Most nights I'm up until morning, but the times I get lucky, I'm able to get about two hours in. I try to be positive throughout every situation I face because I know for a fact nothing is permanent, and I've witnessed what the Most High can do. But I can't lie… PTSD has been kicking my ass.

The grief sometimes was insane. I felt myself being triggered by things I thought I'd healed from. It wasn't easy forgetting all I've been through. I try because I just want to be happy; I know I deserve it. But when I look at the puffiness of my knee, leg, and foot as I struggle to complete normal daily activities and motherly duties, I was always reminded. Sometimes I felt slightly jealous when my friends were able to call on their parents. The feeling of loneliness consumed me.

CHAPTER FIVE

TIED BY BLOOD AND EMOTIONS

I shared a different relationship with each one of my siblings. Krystal is who I saw the most. We supported each other through everything. But when we parted ways at the end of the day, we still both suffered individually. We all did. Krystal was in a relationship that I didn't like, but she was grown, so I had to respect it. I usually always did until it went too far. I know it's best to stay out of people's relationships because they're going to be right back together. But we were all we had. Who would I be to not come to her rescue? I'm not in the best physical situation, but when it was time, that wasn't stopping anything. We've been through too much to let anyone think it was okay to add to it. And when outsiders see that the support system wasn't strong, they try to manipulate the situation, making you think you're all they have. And that's what he did to her. But without a doubt, he knew she had me. Her love life ended up taking a toll on our relationship. I wasn't mad at her; I actually hurt for her. She just wanted to give her baby a two-parent household. An actual mom and dad, something we never had. She wanted love, and it broke my heart hearing her talk about it.

"I know I can take care of myself, and I don't mind being alone, but I'm tired of being alone. I've been like that my whole life. I want to have a relationship. I want to feel loved and be loved sometimes. Shit, we never got that; we never really got a chance to see how it feels. So it be so much and so hard when we do find just a little bit, even if it's toxic. But today just really showed me that that can't be what love feels like," she cried.

And I couldn't judge her because I wanted the same. But what she was experiencing wasn't love. But on the other hand, it may have been the only form of love she's ever felt. And who was I to judge? We only knew love as far as we've experienced it, so we all had our own definition of what it was. And I think the words she said may have explained how I feel as well.

Growing up, Kiara and I were the closest. She was the best big sister ever. She was who I confided in; I told her everything. I remember, like it was yesterday, the first time I got my cycle. I was in elementary school, and it came on when I was in the computer lab. I wasn't feeling well, and when I went to use the bathroom, my underwear was dark and spotty. After getting home, I never told anyone. I was waiting for Kiara to get home. She was in high school and had a job at a music store that she went to straight after school, so I didn't get a chance to see her. I studied the clock until 10 PM that night; that's when she got off. I kept it from my grandma because she was only going to make me feel like it was something I had done wrong and that it was all my fault. She had a way of making me feel guilty about everything.

Kiara finally made it home. I pulled her into the bathroom and showed her my underwear. She made me feel comfortable, and we talked about the things I should expect, but she said we had to tell Grandma. When we told her, she was upset because I had kept it to myself all day. But she never made me feel welcome, so what did she expect?

    Now that I was a young lady, she stopped me from going many places with Kiara. Kiara used to go everywhere, and when she gave birth to Rico, she was in high school, so she didn't get treated as much like a child anymore. She was very mature, even when she was in middle school. After she'd given birth, my grandparents allowed her baby daddy to come around more. I spent a large amount of time with them. Most times when they went to arcades, the mall, movies, etc., I was right there with them. When he bought things for my sister, he would buy for me as well. They never left me out. We established a close bond as time progressed. But the more time I spent with them, the more fond he became of me.

    It was his usual routine to come over every day and spend time with Kiara and Rico, but I grew uncomfortable. One day, he was there and told me to unlock the window so that he could have access to the house later that night. I wanted to tell my sister, but I didn't want him to be mad at me. I never unlocked the window, but the worst thing I could have done was keep it to myself. I'm assuming he unlocked it before he left for the day. The next morning, as we got up to get ready for school, I heard my granddaddy say to my grandma, "The pot of water I had in front of that window is gone; someone poured it out." I sat across from him on the couch, staring at him. I wanted to tell him so badly, but I just couldn't form the words. I didn't understand much of what he was saying at the time, but now that I'm older, I know exactly what he was saying.

He placed big pots of water in front of every window outside of the house, so if someone tried to enter through them, he would know. In order to come in, the water needed to be poured out, or they would step in it. I knew what he was saying because Big Rico got in the house that night, and it had to be through that window since that's where the water was missing from.

I remember my aunt dropping me off at school that morning. I was in middle school, in the 6th grade. My family lived right across the street from my school, and when I got out of the car, my older cousin was standing outside. He was really close to us. He came to my grandparents' home every day. He could see something was wrong with me when I exited the car. "What's wrong, Maj?"

I replied, "Nothing, I'm okay," and continued walking inside the gate. One of my close friends greeted me as I was walking in, and I just burst into tears.

"What's wrong, Majic?"

"Big Rico raped me last night. He snuck in the house and raped me."

"What!"

"You have to go to guidance and tell them," she said. I didn't want to, but she forced me. All I was thinking was that it was my fault because everything was. I didn't want to be the reason my nephew didn't have his dad, and what did that mean for my sister's and my relationship? All of those things ran through my mind, but there was no way I could have kept something like that to myself. My friend and I went to guidance and told the counselor. The deputy came in and listened as well. They called home and told my grandparents to get to the school; it was an emergency.

Seeing my grandparents and sister walking in took my breath away. I loved my sister so much. This was the father of her child; her life had been changed forever. The deputy broke the news. My granddaddy jumped up. "Got damn, Majic, you sat right there this morning and ain't open your mouth! I'm gonna kill that motherfucker!" he yelled.

"Why didn't you tell me this morning?" asked Kiara. "You fixed Rico's bottle; you could've told me then!"

Nobody knew what I was feeling. Nobody understood! I automatically felt I was wrong because I was programmed to have a guilty conscience. There were times I knew I didn't do anything wrong but still felt like I had. The only thing I'd done wrong was adapt to feeling guilty.

We left the guidance office to go to the sexual assault treatment center. We all stood in front of the school while my granddaddy was trying to get it together. Uncle Deon pulled up within three minutes. They weren't handling it well. The school officer asked that they calm down. They got in their car, and I got in the police car to go be examined. The center found his DNA and asked my sister to place a call to him and set him up. I remember him preparing to cross the street at the four-way stop sign as if nothing ever happened the night before. As soon as he stepped into the road, the police closed in on him from each corner.

I was filled with guilt. My nephew lost his dad, and my sister lost her boyfriend. She was young and now a single mother. And you don't just stop loving a person overnight. Soon after, she left for college. She wasn't supposed to go away for school, but it hurt her so badly she wanted to leave. "Are you mad at me?" I asked Kiara as I cried.

She hugged me and replied, "No." But I cried like a baby when she was leaving.

"It's all my fault!" is what I was thinking. Thoughts of the things I could've done differently replayed in my head, and I kept rewinding it. I no longer wanted to defend myself; I just wanted it to be over. If they said I'm lying, okay, I'm lying. When I got on the stand to testify, I was wishing that was the last breath I'd ever take. They asked me sexual questions, and I knew nothing of what they were referring to. The picture they painted of me was all wrong. He told them I was having sex and that I dealt with a lot of guys at school, but I was a virgin.

"Did he come?" the prosecutor asked.

"Come where?" I responded. I was a child. I was the victim! My words wouldn't come out fluently. I was a wreck. "I don't wanna go back," I told Grandma. And she said I didn't have to. She was also saying she was trying to protect us from being removed from her custody. The relief I felt was alleviating. I didn't care what happened and who thought what. And that turned me into the suspect. Throughout the whole ordeal, I was never comforted. But with my grandma telling me I didn't have to go back was the first time I was consoled. I was suffering, but it wasn't safe for me to show it. There was no safe space for me at the time because the situation was sensitive.

The situation strained Kiara's and my relationship as well. I didn't know if she was mad at me or if she was just detached. As time passed, we grew closer, and she became my best friend again. But as a result, we fell out easily. Things that were insignificant had us mad at each other for a while, and it was never that way before. We used to be two peas in a pod. If somebody wanted to fight, we were ready for their ass, even family members. She used to sneak out of the house at night, and I kept all her secrets. She took me on my first date without my grandma ever knowing.

Although Kiara and I had the closest relationship growing up, I think Mya and I related more than I did with the others. Mya had this sadness about her, and so did I. We usually wrote everything down because we were timid, afraid to speak up. Things affected us differently. We were more of the quiet ones, while Krystal and Kiara were outspoken. Growing up, we held a lot in, so it was easier for us to be preyed upon.

Over the years, she became back close with us, but whenever she felt a way, she withdrew from us. Not much would have gone wrong. Mya was mentally messed up, and it seemed as if it would take her the rest of her life to heal from the things she endured. She didn't trust anyone, so it was hard building a healthy relationship with her. A lot of things were a trigger because life for her was horrendous. "Mya, you can't keep pushing us away. We were kids when you were taken away; it was out of our power." Little did we know what was taking place at her dad's house.

"Let's talk about it, Mya. What happened to you over there?"

She cried.

"I barely knew who the man was, but Grandma and Grandaddy assumed he was fit to be a good parent because he came around to spend time with me. I was shy and quiet and barely spoke in the beginning when I moved in with him. Later, I started to warm up to the new change. He was spoiling us, so you can say I became a daddy's girl. I was always up under him because my siblings used to tease me and talk about my mom all the time. They were very mean to me and made my sister and me fight constantly. When he let me come over to see y'all, I always felt welcomed. Soon after, he started making my sister come with me when I came over so she could watch me. One day, I asked Grandma when I could come back to stay with y'all, and my sister went back and told. He then stopped me from coming over like I used to because he didn't like how I told you guys everything. But soon, I was going to find out why. My sister and I had to sleep in the bed with him every night until my oldest brother moved out. We then shared a room together; I had the top bunk, and she had the bottom. That's when she and I became close and started to play together more often, but somehow it was always competition between us.

My dad was a good dad in the beginning, but that was just an act to get us to gravitate closer to him. He completely stopped both my sister and me from speaking with our family on our mom's side. He made it seem like they really didn't care about us and that they didn't love us like they said they did. He used to say, "Out of sight, out of mind," meaning that if I'm not with them or calling them, then they weren't worried about me. Grandma and Grandaddy were my heart, and he knew how much I loved them; he also knew they were my weakness. I used to have to sneak to call y'all and erase the number from the call log. He made my sister and me do everything together, and we went everywhere together because he knew we would always tell on each other. My dad was known for being one of the best dads raising all his kids on his own, and everybody looked up to that. He put us in cheerleading and my brothers in football at the local park when I was 9 years old. He was also the football coach, but cheering became my life. I cheered for little league for 7 years and in middle school for 2 years. We then ended up making the cut for the All-Star Traveling Cheerleading Competition Squad a while later. Life was semi-good, despite the fact that I could barely talk to y'all anymore unless he called sporadically. Even though my brothers, sister, and I grew up in the same house, we were very much divided. My dad played everything right from the beginning; he made sure we never really got close. My brothers stayed at the park, and my sister and I stayed trapped inside. He made us cook for them every night, clean the entire house every day, wash everybody's clothes, and do outside work like pulling weeds from the rocks, raking leaves, washing the cars, and even taking care of our newborn baby sister as if she were ours. It was almost like he was turning my sister and me into his housewives. He had a girlfriend, who is my baby sister's mom. We never really got along with each other. I don't know why she felt like she was in competition with a 10-year-old at the time, but she said she didn't like how I was always up under my dad and how I still slept in his bed. Now, anybody else would've questioned that, but she didn't. Every Sunday night was family movie night in that house, and the first one to fall asleep had to go to bed. This particular Sunday night, she, her son, and the rest of us watched a movie in the den after dinner. I was always the first person to fall asleep and was sent to bed. But that night, instead of him picking me up and taking me to my bed like he always did, he let me stay there asleep until the movie was over, even after everyone else left for the night and went to bed.

He then picked me up and took me to his bed and told me how I wasn't bathing myself right, so he was going to teach me. He took my clothes off and put his mouth down there to my vagina and started licking it. I was shaking uncontrollably and felt weird, I knew it was something not right about that. At that age, I didn't know what he was doing was wrong. I had no mom or anyone else to tell me about it, so I thought it was truth in what he was saying. I thought that's how fathers clean their daughters like he said. It continued repeatedly. After that, as months went by, he started making me put his penis in my mouth and told me to suck it. By the time I turned 11 years old, and got my first period, he started penetrating me. I lost my virginity to my father! I was bleeding and crying and knew something bad was happening. All he had to say was that it was normal and other men have sex with their daughter's and even marry them. After that day, a movie on lifetime came on about how a father was raping his daughter and had a relationship with her. The mother found out and killed him. That day is when I knew that what my dad was doing was wrong. Soon after the abuse started, he threatened to kill grandma and I and said nobody would even care.

He kept up the "all-time greatest father" image outside of the house, but he was the devil behind closed doors. I constantly went to school with huge bruises on my body. One day my friend went to tell the counselor and they called the Child Protective Services. I was terrified to tell the truth because of the constant threats, so I lied, and the people actually believed me! After multiple calls for the same reason, they still didn't notice a terrified child in an unstable home. I started fighting back and crying, every night he made me sleep in his bed to rape me. He used to make me go to school sometimes in the dirty clothes I wore the day before if I fought back. I became very insecure and self-conscious. Not only was I being raped and abused at home, I was also being bullied by kids at school. Students used to constantly call me big nose Mya and picked on the way I walked. I used to even get beat up by these 2 little boys and never once said anything. I got held back in the 3rd grade because I was told I couldn't read and comprehend and that was the first year FCAT became apart of the curriculum.

That gave students another reason to bully me. Reality for me wanted to go home to escape the bullying at school, but then go to school to escape the rape and abuse at home. At that point, all I learned to do was fight. I would fight just so I wouldn't get messed with anymore. And it became a way to release the built up pain I was going through at home. One day, I pulled my sister to the side and asked her was daddy raping her too, because he showed me a video of her sucking his penis. She said no and went and told him exactly what I said. My punishment was a beating followed by him raping me again while saying "I can't believe you asked her that. If anything you should've asked was I making love to her because that is what I'm doing."

    I couldn't trust her with anything after that and I felt all alone because I knew I had no one to talk to. A few nights later, my dad, sister, and I went to Winn-Dixie, he left us in the car while he went to go grab something.

    My sister then brought up the time I asked her about daddy raping her and I told her that he was doing that to me and I wanted to know if the same thing happened to her. She said it was happening to her too and that she was just scared to talk about it. When we got back home that night, we sat down and talked about everything together. She told me how he had been penetrating her ever since she was 10 years old because she had gotten her period early at age 9. She was more hurt that it was happening to me because she was the one who was supposed to be protecting me. Ever since that day, we have been protecting each other. He would just randomly come take one of us every night and the more we fought back the more physical he became. It was days he came in the room and just pulled me from the top bunk and I fell on my face onto the floor. My sister would wake up some nights if she heard him grabbing me and ask him to leave me alone, he would either leave or take her instead. He used to tell us that he would get both of us in the room one day and have a 3-some with each other. He used to let us go to his mom's house often for the weekends to go to church with her. It used to be her, my sister, my 3 brothers and I sleeping in her big bed. I was in the middle and my brother was at the foot of me. One started to get touchy and began feeling on my private parts. He then stuck his finger in my vagina. I told my grandmother. He denied it and she didn't even believe me. She thought I was making up lies to get him in trouble because he was the main one to bother me and pick on me. After that, I never said anything else. I just let it happen and what was only touching soon turned into him raping me when no one was home. He used to tell me how much he loved having sex with me. Not long after, he went to prison for 4 years. There were only two brothers left in the house and my sister.

My dad never stopped raping us. When I was 13 years old, he thought he got me pregnant, he beat me so bad like he was trying to beat it out of me. I started bleeding really bad down there. Another time, he had one of his side chicks take me to the clinic and told her I was out there having sex with boys.

In middle school, my 8th grade year, my sister and I were temporarily removed from his custody. We were sent to live with my fraternal grandmother due to all the allegations that were built up against him. Even though he was ordered not to be around us, my grandmother still allowed him to come over. He used to pick us up one by one and take us to this ducked off lake by the high school y'all went to. Or he would rape us while in her house when she wasn't there. He even did it one time I was on my period. I always had really bad menstrual cramps, and that left me in even more pain.

His mom was mentally crazy and controlling. She swore she changed her life over to God, but she was just a hypocrite. Later down the line, I would find out the truth behind her ways and her reasons.

While staying with her, I was able to catch the bus to come and see y'all like every other day. That was the only good thing about the temporary move. I loved seeing y'all, and all the family. I knew I just belonged with y'all. Soon As I thought everything was getting better, I found out granddaddy had cancer. It was said that he's been fighting it a while, but when aunt Tracy's husband hit him in the head, he spiraled downhill from there. When he passed away, my dad didn't even allow me to go to his funeral. I was devastated! And even more hurt when I found out that my his mom went, but I couldn't even go. Not long after, I found out grandma had been fighting cancer. This time, after granddaddy died, the cancer had spread throughout her body and she started to lose her hair and a lot of weight. I used to break down crying because I hated to see her like that, and I didn't want to lose her. While being over there all the time, I got really close to you. I was already close with Krystal and Jr. because we were around the same age. Grandma was getting sicker and sicker, she called me in the room one day and asked was my dad touching me in the wrong way. I didn't want her to worry about anything like that while she was already fighting for her life, so I told her no. But she knew I was lying.

When my sister turned 16 years old, she ran away and left me alone in the house with that man. I found out that she had been talking to ChildNet and her mom, and she told them enough of the story to get away. I was so mad at her and couldn't believe she left without me and when Child Protective Services came to speak with me about the allegations, I lied because I hated her for that. We were both still going to the same High School, but she was in foster care and had gotten adopted. She stopped me one day and asked me why did I lie to the people because that was my way of getting out. She told me that she sent them back to get me and all I had to do was tell the truth. I felt so bad and stupid at the same time to even think that she was going to leave me in a situation like that. That same year, grandma passed away, and I felt like the world officially came down on me. I begged my dad to let me go to her funeral and he did. I was depressed for weeks after grandma passed. Furthermore, I had suicidal thoughts and even thoughts of killing my dad. I wasn't mentally stabled and thought I had become somehow like our mom. One day, my older cousin had been following me home from school so he knew I would be alone. He came to the house and I let him in. Not knowing that he was coming in there to rape me, and what started as the one time became a continuous thing. He used to rape me and then throw money at me like I was some type of prostitute. He told me that he and my dad both used to have sex with our mama when she was high on drugs, and he used to throw the money at her too.

Soon after, my other brother and I became really close because we were the last two who remained in the house. The next year, when I turned 17 years old, I ended up telling him everything that daddy had been doing to me and since he had just turned 18 years old a month earlier, my dad was ready to kick him out. One day, while in the backyard, my same brother came to me and said he knew that I wasn't lying about my other brother touching me and having sex with me because he told him. He then said he wanted to do the same thing to me that he did. At that point I just didn't even fight anymore, I just let them do whatever they wanted to do to me. I felt like I was a sex slave to my whole family and I couldn't escape it. My dad told me that once my brother leaves, he can finally get me pregnant and raise the baby with me. He said he would just tell everybody that I had sex with some boy, and he left me. I knew I had to get away and never look back, so I called y'all, and we started planning to run away.

My baby sister asked my dad why did it look like I was packing, and for the next 2 days my dad didn't go to work. I had to change my plans and leave everything behind, so the next day after school, you picked me up and drove me to the police station. That's when I told the detectives a verbatim of everything that happened since I was 10 years old. They would rather not continue on with the investigation because they said it were so many allegations and every time they asked us, we lied. I told them we lied because we were scared and every time my dad was there just looking at us as if he were going to kill us if me even made eye contact. So even after all that, he never paid for what he's done to me.

I was speechless! There wasn't a number that existed for the number of tears I cried for her. I couldn't believe what I just heard. No wonder, trust was the last thing on her mind! The very person who supposed to been protecting her, hurt her the worst. That was disgusting! Nasty ass fuck nigga! That shit was unfathomable!

We were all just a bunch of broken kids mimicking adult lives. My little brother Jr was out here searching for love through women. When one didn't work, he was with someone new the following week. He couldn't be alone. He was searching for a love he knew existed but was yet to feel.

We all suffered in our way. We all dealt with our things. None was more important than the other because no one knew the will power it took for each of us to get through whatever we were going through. We didn't have the same strength. What one may have lacked in, the other may have shown more strength. And being there for one another sometimes wasn't possible. The mental toll things took on me, isolation became my way of coping. My mind and heart couldn't take it, no matter how good my intentions were. But There was one thing we all had in common and that was our blood and emotions.

CHAPTER SIX

ITS COMPLICATED

There were many times I'd ask myself, "Why don't Nick ever come to the hospital?" It wasn't like we weren't on speaking terms. But one thing he did after a falling out was hold out on his expression. At times, it would be awkward for me to bring up something like that if we weren't on that type of timing at the moment. But I think regardless of whether we were or not, we had a friendship and a connection that couldn't be denied. I would think it had something to do with me being with Jason when the accident occurred. Even though he came to visit when I was in Georgia, I still felt that way.

There was a time I was going on a date, and he asked me, "Who are you going with?" But I acted like it was a secret. It wasn't a secret; it's just that some things are awkward to mention to one another, but we still did it when we wanted to play the game of seeing if the other one cared or not. "Okay, remember what happened last time you was with a nigga and didn't tell me? Now look at how life is," he replied. I was appalled. I'm like, no, this nigga didn't! But I also recognized that he was in his feelings.

I laughed and responded, "I did tell you. I told you I was going out of town with my friend. And yeah, I might have to do things a little different, but it ain't stopping shit. Shit still getting done." He definitely had me fucked up!

"Okay, I was just making sure you were safe, that's all," he replied. But yeah, nigga, don't play with me!

On the other hand, I gave him the guy's name. There was another time we were in the car going to Miami, and he brought the situation up again. "You know I was so mad at you when I got that call?" And once again, he said I didn't tell him. But I know I did. I damn near tell him everything because he was always on my mind. I didn't say much on it this time because I didn't want to talk about it. I thought to myself for a while if I should ask him if it made him feel a way that I was with a guy when everything transpired. I was conflicted to ask because anytime he felt uncomfortable, he acted stupid. Instead of expressing himself, he'd try to pretend he didn't know what I was talking about, then blow things out of proportion.

When I was in the hospital, Ebony called. "Did Nick come?"

"Girl, no," I said in an agitated manner.

"I think it may make him feel one way or another to see you in that situation," she said.

"It probably makes him sad that I'm still going through this, but he doesn't want to bring it up because he doesn't want to accidentally offend me. Lord knows I didn't want to ask him."

I did, but I knew this man like the back of my hand, and he'll never admit to feeling a way because if you don't care in such a way, how can you be mad, right? But I really wanted to know because we just acted like it wasn't there. All these scars, but it was something we ignored. He never asked about surgeries or what was happening next. Maybe it just didn't bother him because he still loved me the same. But it was pulling on my brain until I decided to ask.

Me: "Why you won't show up for me the way I do for you? It almost seems as if you're holding something against me the way your actions fluctuate."

Nick: "What do you mean show up for you? I am right here messaging you to make sure the surgery went well. I messaged you a couple of times at work when you were about to go and do the surgery you didn't tell me about. I feel like you are just saying something to just say something right now. Saying that you feel like I was holding something against you—holding something against you for what? We are friends; friends can't hold anything against each other, so I don't understand it. And as far as attitude fluctuating, you and I would bump heads, or you would stay doing something."

Me: "You always say friends can't do this and that, but they can. Friends are also a relationship. Friends have more differences than people in a romantic relationship. I always asked you if I was overstepping. Many things made me feel like it was okay to do or say because you would come that way, and that's the relationship we have. Now I'm seeing that's where the imbalance comes in due to us always falling out. So now I see I have been overstepping. I will make adjustments."

But what did I expect? I knew he was going to handle it exactly the way he did. Even though I predicted it, I can't say he didn't hurt my feelings a bit. After that, I told myself to just back off. Which I did. Our conversation became brief, sometimes nothing at all. About three weeks later, he FaceTimed me, smiling on the other end, standing in a kitchen of what seemed to be a hollow apartment. He moved into his new place, showing me with excitement. And even though things were what they were between us, I was happy for him. We planned to meet up a few days ago, but I had been busy. Truth be told, I just wasn't making him a priority anymore. The way I usually rearranged time for him was no longer happening.

Me: "I'm gonna try to meet up with you later tomorrow. Make arrangements."

Nick: "I've been waiting on you."

Me: "I've been busy; I'll let you know when and where."

Nick: "Okay, cool."

Me: (later that night) "Meet me at my sister's house. Not at this moment. I'll let you know when I'm on my way."

Nick: "You wanna bring it to my house

Me: "I'll let you know when to send the address."

Nick: "Okay."

Me: "Send it." (a couple of hours later).

A few moments after he sent his location, I turned in and told him to come to the front. There was a guard gate, and since I wasn't sent a physical address, I couldn't go exactly where the map was taking me. After deciding to park in front of the rent office, I backed my car in, filled with nervousness. I hadn't seen him in a while.

To think about it, we had been showing our ass badly towards each other. He pulled up next to me. On the inside, I was smiling, but I washed all traces of it away as he approached my car. I gave him his things, pulling off immediately after. My throat locked, and I became anxious, swallowing hard. I thought of so many things I wanted to say, but I was rushed with so many emotions, not knowing what step was appropriate to take next. Before I could make it out of the gate, he texted.

"I asked you if you wanted to just bring it so that you could also see my place and know where I'm at since you have been being good."

The times he said I've been being good were the times I was cool off his ass. Most likely, it was a time he made me feel a way, so I cut all contact, trying to let go.

"But you didn't tell me what to do when I came in; I told you I was turning in." The way he responded, I could tell he felt dismissed, and it was about to go left, so I turned around. It was obvious he missed me, and even though I tried to hide it, I missed him just as much. That nigga was so fine; I don't even know why I set myself up like that. When I pulled back in, he was out front waiting for me. I followed him until we made it to his place. As we got out of the car, he held my hand to assist me in walking up the stairs.

We were each other's addiction, with half parts pleasure and equal parts pain. After making it upstairs, he showed me around. It was satisfying to see him growing positively.

He told me he thought of me when he picked out his couch. It was a recliner, and I appreciated that because usually, when I visited someone's home, I was uncomfortable. After a short while, my leg needed to be elevated. If I wasn't comfortable enough with the person, I wasn't going to put my feet on their couch, just out of respect.

We sat down and began to catch up. I started to tell him about my upcoming event and the decor I was going for. I mentioned the attire, which was a formal dress code. "You need to be the rawest nigga in the building," I blushed. But I didn't expect anything less from him. I wanted him to be my date, but I didn't want to ask. I could tell he was thinking the same. He started to bring up other niggas, but he just didn't know how close he was to my heart. I dated, but none of those niggas were seeing him. I played it cool, though. We stayed on dumb shit, playing in each other's face, but we had about one month to figure it out.

I was there for a while before it was time for me to leave to take Krystal something to eat. She recently had given birth to her first child, a little girl, and was unable to leave the house. He walked me outside, holding my hand until we made it down the stairs. He opened the door for me to get in the car. We awkwardly stared into each other's eyes, not knowing what our next move should be. "Maj, look, you see my new car?" he said, breaking the silence.

In my head, I'm thinking, "OH MY FUCKING GOSH!" but instead, I surprisingly said, "Dang, you ain't tell me or nothing." We both laughed. But truth be told, I already knew.

There was this spot I frequently drove past while I was on the road. Anytime I made it right there, I thought of him. Years ago, he called me after being away on business. This particular time, I was so worried after not hearing from him; it was unusual. I was on the phone with Keyshia before his call came in. "Girl, you ain't hear from him yet?" she asked.

"Girl, no," I responded sadly. But as soon as I said that, I had another incoming call. I remember it so well because of the anticipation he and I shared. I was smiling so hard, happy to hear from him.

"Hey, Maj, you miss me?" I did so much.

"Yes," I said, while blushing. He began to tell me what was

going on.

Moving forward, a couple of months ago, as soon as I made it to that exact spot in the road, I was cut off by a car I'd never seen before. I was big on paying attention on the road and to my surroundings; I stayed on beat. I was a car lover, so I'm like, "Damn, what is that?" There weren't too many cars I was unfamiliar with. But for some reason, I had never seen this one before, and I'm like, "Damn, that shit is raw as fuck!"

But the car cutting me off is what stood out to me. It was meant for me. It came out of nowhere; I didn't see it coming. And the funny part about it is that I knew it had a deeper meaning. The universe often sent me confirmations and downloads. The synchronicities between Nick and me were scary. But the dreams were even scarier. So when it cut me off, instead of becoming upset, I just smiled and said, "Nick has that car." Me and him weren't on speaking terms before my surgery, so I wasn't aware. "Oh my gosh, he has that car!" I screamed to myself, smiling. As I'm going around the corner, I see another one exactly like it, so I'm even more convinced he has it. I was in such a good mood because the telepathy was undeniable. "I can't believe he didn't even tell me!" But I was happy for him. I wanted to text and say congratulations, but I had second thoughts like, "What if he really doesn't have that car?" And besides, in our last conversation, he told me to leave him alone for good.

So when he just pointed the car out to me, I was really screaming on the inside. I couldn't believe it. I just smiled and said it was nice. At this point, our eyes were locked without saying a word. Once again, I broke the silence while saying goodnight as I backed away. When I looked in my rearview mirror, he was standing in the road, still watching me drive away. The emotion was high. I smiled for the remainder of the night.

CHAPTER SEVEN

THE IMPORTANCE OF A FATHER

I went to my daddy's house and stretched out on the couch. He came downstairs, and we began laughing and joking. If you knew us, that was our usual routine. The neighbors were going to hear us because he laughed just as loud as I did.

My dad and I's relationship was going steadily. He'd been helping me look for venues for my writing event and told all of his friends about it. I was great at writing; many people knew it. They were always asking me for a project. After the accident was the perfect time, but that wasn't an easy task. I started when I came back from Georgia in 2019, but I was more focused on healing. Every time I began, I stopped. It wasn't something I could commit to at the time. I couldn't excel the way I wanted to because my main focus was my mobility. Learning to walk again was my biggest priority. As the years progressed, I was healing great. I was stable, and everything was everything. I started back writing, and it all came together and flowed gracefully. I mentioned taking my writing seriously to Krystal, Ebony, and my daddy; they all were very supportive, as well as motivational at the times I doubted myself. I was still on the fence about it because I would have to speak on things I wasn't quite ready for. I didn't want to rub anyone the wrong way; I just wanted to speak my truth. But there's no way I could have told the good without telling the bad. I began talking to numerous people who were close to my mom and around her and my dad. Many said he was the worst thing that ever happened to her. And it didn't come from my immediate family; they always spared me because he was my father. I didn't want to hurt anyone, but I couldn't stop the calling the Most High had on my life. My purpose was to motivate the world. My words were something special. The gift was mine when He created me in my mother's womb. I was the sacrificial lamb for my family and for everyone who shared some of my similar experiences. Many are too ashamed, so I was chosen to relay the message.

I cooked Sunday dinner and invited my dad over. The menu included ribs, macaroni and cheese, sweet cornbread, collard greens, and rice. As he was eating his food, we sparked up a conversation. A lot of emotions of frustration were expressed. He felt like I'd been through a lot and I needed to tell my story. I said, "Well, I'll start it after the accident."

"No, but you can't do that; you're leaving too much out." And I realized I really couldn't do that because so much had taken place before it—some things I thought I would have never made it out of. I'm sure he assumed everything would be about my maternal side of the family because of the way he felt about them. It was true they played a role in some of my pain, but no one owed me more than what my parents did. So he was held to a higher standard. I knew I was going to have to talk about the role he played in my mom's life and the role he didn't play in mine. And I was honestly not trying to deal with all that. I knew he would feel a way. But after our conversation that night, he made me feel like he was going to be okay with it. That night is when I planted it in my heart that I was going through with it, and I was going to finish it. He knew I was talking to family and friends regarding my mom's drug addiction. My oldest sister, Kiara, she knew a lot. I had some vivid memories, but she could tell you who made her cry when she was three months old. He started telling me his version of how she got on drugs, but it was some stuff I'd never even heard before. I started asking around to different people, and it was proven that he was lying. When it came closer to my event, I kept reassuring my dad that no one should be mad. This is my story and how it affected me. No one could be mad for the emotions I harbored. His feedback was always as if he was one hundred percent excluded from my emotional distress. Time was ticking. He would come with me to check out venues. I needed to lock something in ASAP. After deciding, we kept going back so the decorators could plan their setup. I put the finishing touches on my project, completely finishing it. My stomach was in knots, but I was proud of myself. I couldn't believe it. I did that shit! There was no going back after this. I wasn't even sure if Nick would be okay with it, but it was a chance I was willing to take. My story was insignificant without him. It showed the world that unconditional love did exist.

After submission, the company was in amazement. Every day until my event, she quoted something I said and put it on social media. She told me, "I've worked with many people, but this by far is the best one." She even changed the requirements for her other upcoming projects. She started giving me different roles, and I was new.

Ebony, Erica, my daddy, and his girlfriend were giving their opinions. They helped with decisions a lot, but I was extremely strategic and tedious, so I always ended up doing what felt right to me. October first found its way to my front door, and "nervous" was an understatement! I didn't sleep at all the night before. Changing my mind was a battle, but I put in too much work to turn away now. That project took me through it. I dreaded finishing many times. It put me in a constant state of depression. The anguish weighed a ton. So many times, I said "fuck it" while writing it. Reliving that trauma wasn't easy, but I'm not a quitter. I pushed through the pain, and my purpose was born.

I anticipated each new day as the sun crept in through my window. I was finally living for something that was mine and couldn't be taken away from me. My life had been lived strictly for my daughters, so happiness wasn't something I experienced often from others. But now, my existence felt meaningful. It was a high that never vanished. It was a familiar feeling, similar to the rebirth celebration I had a few months ago. I rented out the conference room at Capital Grille, a fine dining restaurant. I celebrated life and all I'd gained over the past three years. As I walked in, the staff clapped and cheered me on. My daddy and Krystal both were by my side to escort me in. They opened the double doors, and the room was filled with my family and friends. The attire was red and black, as I requested. There was a projector displaying a slideshow of me and my progress. I shed tears as I watched. That shit was hard! The surgeries, continuing to bounce back mentally—the smell of the wounds, the scars—everything about it was challenging. It was the hardest thing I've ever experienced. And as I watched the display, I was still going through it, trying to fully recover. It showed me in every aspect you could think of: swollen, frail, depressed, exhausted, bald-headed, crying, in pain. But it ended with me laughing, dancing in the club, spoiling my daughters, drop-dead gorgeous, as my uncle Tim would call me, walking around without my walker. Raw as fuck! And I did it all alone. In some instances, that was good, but in most cases, it wasn't. Now I felt like I didn't need anybody. Little did I know, it was just the beginning of a monster being created.

Nick, the girls, and I stepped out of the car clean as a whistle. My silver sequined dress was draped in the front with a plunging neckline. My waist was out, and the back crisscrossed, met in the middle where it tied. A split came up my right thigh, revealing my skin graft scar a little. My shoes were silver with a clear strap across the toe and silver stones covering the heels. There were silver straps coming up my ankle.

Nick matched me with a silver and black suit and silver Giuseppe casual shoes. The girls both wore beautiful long white formal dresses with little silver kitten heels. Many of my guests were standing outside, waiting for me to pull up. As soon as we stepped out of the car, they flooded us with pictures. Walking inside, there was a massive knot in my throat; I couldn't even swallow. My heart was beating fast, but I reminded myself that everyone who was there was in attendance for me. I walked through the doors of the room with greetings from everyone, followed by a standing ovation. They all were clapping and cheering me on. The feeling was indescribable. Even though I planned it, it was all done for me. They were all there to see me. There were even people there I didn't know. The room was beautiful, exactly what I had in mind. The food was set up in the back, with the servers standing behind the table. The menu consisted of salmon, chicken breast, mashed potatoes, a vegetable medley mixed with cauliflower, broccoli, and carrots, dinner rolls, and a cake with vanilla glaze icing. The room was satisfying to see, filled with purple and silver decor. The stage was embellished just for me. There were posters of me on both ends of the stage, supported by an easel, and in the middle was my table with a white and silver tablecloth. The chairs were covered in silver sequined chair covers and purple bow ties. There were white, silver, and black draping behind me, with purple lights reflecting from them. I made my way to the stage, but I was having a hard time getting up there. Now that I think about it, I went up the wrong way. My little brother Jr. was already on the stage, waiting to assist me. He pulled me up after the struggle I was having.

He and his girlfriend came from Georgia; I felt complete with his presence. My siblings and I didn't have the best relationship, but there was a thrill we all felt when one or the other accomplished something great. The way we were treated because of my mom will never sit well with us. People can try to convince themselves we weren't treated any differently, but my sisters, brother, and I knew what it was. And every time I think about it, I just want to shit on a bitch even harder. When we stuck together, we weren't shit to be played with. None of us!

It was time for the program to start. The guests got up to speak on my behalf, one at a time. Many of them stated how they knew me and said really nice things. Kim got up and spoke from a mother's point of view, letting me know how proud she was of me. Keyshia came into town just for my event, and I really appreciated that. She cried as she spoke, but I understood. Me and her had been through some shit! Just thinking of the nights we were on an all-night flight, not sleeping for days, making shit happen like real girls do. When Jr. got up and grabbed the mic, I instantly became emotional before he got the chance to say a word. Nobody understood the importance of this like we did.

"Hello, for the ones that don't know me, that's my sister. I'm her youngest brother. Whew!......I have a book to tell too! Sis, I'm proud of you. Let me start off by saying that. We were the ones who were always counted out! But look, we proved to stand on top!" He began to cry and finished with, "Just know Grandma and Grandaddy are proud of you!" He put the mic down and walked towards me. I stood up out of my seat, and we began to hug and share a few tears. I don't cry easily, but that was personal.

Shortly after, my guests started lining up to get their personal autographs and take pictures with me. I was having the time of my life. We laughed endlessly, sang, and danced a little. I have a natural high, so I never cared who was watching. The line died down, and Nick and the girls were now approaching. I signed his book and took pictures with them. He looked too good. That was my first time seeing him in that kind of attire, but he wore the hell out of it. All night, my family was telling me how clean he was. My cousin said he was the best dressed in the building.

I saw people in attendance I went to school with whom I hadn't seen in years. There was this guy named Kirk; he had a crush on me since middle school. Kirk was 5'7", caramel complexion, long dreads, VVs in his mouth; he wore a lot of jewelry, very much the flashy type. He was there with another guy I had never seen before. When they made their way to the stage, the homeboy put his hands around my waist and whispered in my ear, "Girl, you fine as a motherfucker." My immediate reaction was to jump back a little. I wasn't trying to be rude, but I didn't know him, and he was all in my personal space. I could tell he had been drinking a lot prior to the event. And one thing about Nick, he'll act like he's not looking, but he's watching everything. He was my date that night, and I never wanted him to feel disrespected. Kirk told his friend to chill after I nudged him away. As I signed Kirk's book, he stood in front of me, smiling. "Got damn, Majic! Girl, you so beautiful. I'm proud of you for real." After I handed them their merchandise, they gave me far more than the cost.

I made thousands of dollars that night, and it was just the beginning. The night came to an end. We started to clean the place while everyone was participating. But some were still asking to take pictures. Keyshia took a picture of me and Kirk at his request, "since we didn't get one earlier on stage," is what he said. She smiled the whole time behind the camera, but it was innocent. "My friend is really that girl; y'all got her fucked up! Y'all look good as fuck together; I love him for you," Keyshia said. We both began to laugh. Everyone knew Keyshia didn't give a fuck about anything, and she had no filter. Her roster consisted of about ten niggas, and she was always scoping for number eleven. It wasn't in her nature to deal with only one guy. And if she still stuck around after finding out about another female, she was going to dog his ass out. That's why she didn't care much for Nick and my relationship. She felt like he took me for granted. She didn't know him personally, but she knew of the situation. And she knew back then he had the ability to get me in my feelings bad.

The times he didn't run and was present, she loved that for me. It's safe to say that she only wanted what wanted me, and I loved her for that. As the night came to an end, the girls left with Kim, and Nick took me home.

I ordered three hundred books for the night, and I went home with a quarter of what I purchased. I felt a little discouraged because I was hoping to sell out. But little did I know, there were people supporting me all over the world. I delivered the remainder of the books that were left the next day, and I completely sold out of everything by the end of the night. For the customers I couldn't get to, I redirected them to Amazon for their purchase. Soon after, I sold every book that Amazon had in stock. I was crying tears of joy. I couldn't believe it. I knew I had a fan base, but I was a loner, so I was a bit surprised. Quite often, I underestimated myself. I needed more books as soon as possible! There were orders coming in left and right! I quickly ordered more. I was making trips to the shipping center every single day. I was shipping to about ten different states, and I knew it was only going to get better.

I was exhausted! It was time to go home to lay down. My leg and ankle had become swollen, and I was having an extreme amount of pain from sitting in the car too long. It needed to be elevated, but it was imminent that I delivered those books. People were waiting on me. After my shower, I rested for the remainder of the day. Flipping through the channels, my phone went off…

Kirk: "I started reading your book at 8 this morning, and I just now finished it. I have a damn crook in my neck because I couldn't put it down. The crazy part is that's my first book I've read since high school… ahhhh mannn, it's so much to take in, shit felt like a Tyler Perry movie. What's crazy is that I always followed your story before the book because your accident happened on my birthday. Over the years, I watched the progression of what you put out there, even your close ones' content. While I was celebrating for life, you were fighting for life, and that always stuck with me. I constantly had feelings of reaching out but didn't want to feel like a groupie, I guess. Or even one of those people that came around just to be nosy. But I'm blessed that you shared your story, and even though it feels like a book that will grab women's attention, for me as a man, it definitely hit me because certain areas you touched on, I can relate to. Like heavily, and plus I used to be a hoe. I never knew how that could scar women until I read your story. You make me want to call each one of them and apologize, and which eventually I will if I ever get the opportunity to again. But for real, your book has so much to talk about and so many points that you shared that I don't even know where to start."

I was elated! For my book to touch a man in such a way was something I never expected. Him wanting to be a better person because of me was intriguing, simply because these days men didn't seem to take how they left women feeling into consideration. I ain't even gonna lie; I found the accountability attractive.

My book was doing well. It was trending on social media and in the streets. The girl Steve was cheating on me with when I was pregnant with Zuri even reached out to me. She saw people kept talking about it, and she asked for details on purchasing. Money was money, and the business me and Steve had was over. We didn't even co-parent.

She sent me her location to drop off her book. I got in my car and headed her way. While I was en route, Steve called. I saw his number pop up, and I'm like, what the fuck? Because it was out of the ordinary.

Me: "Hello?"

Steve: "Hello? What's up? I just wanted to say congratulations, and I'm proud of you. I know how much you love to write, and I wanted to tell you to keep doing what you're doing. I love you, and I always will."

Me: "Thank you; I really appreciate it."

If I said I expected that, I'd be lying. It felt weird talking to him; that's how distant we were. At one point, it was us against the world. That's what we always said to each other. I didn't have anyone, and he and Kim would have just had this huge fight, so it would feel like it was just that "us against the world." And the way we made shit happen, we didn't need anyone else. But times had changed tremendously. I wasn't an enemy because when his girlfriend wasn't around, he'd try to speak and be friendly. But when she was around, he wanted her to believe he hated me. And that's what the girl knew; that's why he wasn't allowed to talk to me. Either way, I didn't give a fuck. That was the least of my concerns. He changed so much, such as his morals, and the father he once was. That was her man now. I didn't want any parts.

I smiled as we hung up the phone. I really appreciated the call because, like he said, if no one else knew, he knew how much I loved to write. That was my passion. And he knew I was lit with it. In middle school, he used to watch all my homeboys come to me to write poetry for their girlfriends. That call was big of him, and I respected his act of kindness. It put me in an even better mood.

"Hello, I'm outside," I said as I pulled up to the girl's house. I made my way to her door, waiting for her to come out. I usually don't get out of the car, but she needed to see this here pressure. My hair was done, nails, lashes, and brows. My skin was pretty as fuck and glowing, not a spot in sight. And the body was bodying.

"Hey, thank you for coming. I'm going to let you know what I think as soon as I start reading. I'm about to take a shower, then I'm going to start." "Okay, no problem, keep me posted," I responded.

She was staring at me, and I couldn't help but smile. I knew I was that girl. The fact that she fucked my man and continued to fuck him while I was home with our kids, most likely crying or waiting for him to get there, felt rewarding. Whether she knew it or not, she helped me find myself. I'll never forget that while Steve was fucking with her, he told me, "Single mothers are the strongest women." He told me that to make me feel bad about myself.

He used to try to tear me down a lot because I suffered from depression. He knew that his words could get to me, and he said it to justify his cheating, in other words saying I was weak. He failed to realize that I wasn't a single mother, so I shouldn't have to act as one. I was supposed to be able to bask in my femininity. He was the provider, but he would try to make me feel bad for him providing. His attempt failed. The only thing he made me do was want to become a single mother. Ever since that day, I began to picture myself alone. I started seeing images in the back of my mind of me in my own place. My visions were vivid and kept becoming clearer. I was there in the physical, but mentally I was long gone. It wasn't her fault because she didn't owe me any loyalty, but she contributed to my demise. So to know I came out of that, been through hell and back, and was still standing in front of her, beautiful as fuck, and she couldn't touch me with a ten-foot pole felt wonderful! She had a shape, but it was far beyond that for me. I was a beautiful person from the inside out. I exuded radiance. And I knew it. So I walked like it and talked like it. Nobody could ever think they were going to talk to me crazy or treat me in such a way that didn't align with the woman I presented myself to be. Most of all, there was no malice in my heart, and I loved that for me. I handed her my book and walked away.

Trips to FedEx, UPS, and the post office became my new norm. The thing I loved most about it was that it kept me on the run. Usually, my mind ran nonstop, but this wasn't the time to let my thoughts consume me. The reviews poured in. When I went on social networks, I would see my book posted in a row across the top as my supporters bragged about it. There were people crying because it reminded them of their childhood or a situation they were living in at the moment. I was really out here helping people. Amazon was now filled with five-star reviews. I never could have predicted this. Something so complex gave the world hope to continue their fight.

The last time I heard from my dad was two days after the event. I spoke to him briefly, but I could tell by his lack of enthusiasm that something was bothering him. Immediately, I knew the reason why.

His girlfriend called a few days later. "Majic, I'm on chapter five, and oh my gosh! This book is amazing!" "I've been laughing and crying my eyes out as well." "Girl, you are a miracle, and I'm extremely proud of you." "Look at all that you've overcome; look at the way you care for and take care of the girls." If no one else has ever said it, I'm here to tell you I am." My heart was filled with joy.

"My dad hasn't been answering the phone for me," I said. "Oh, he's just been tired and resting a lot lately." But I knew better. He would've checked on me by now to see how the book sales were going. My main focus was to tell my story, not to validate anyone's feelings. No one could tell me that the way I felt was wrong. No one had the means to tell me what I've endured wasn't that serious because we all suffer differently. I didn't feel I wronged him, so there was nothing to apologize for. But Uncle Tim thought otherwise. He called me in tears, "You owe your dad an apology, sweetheart." When it came to my Uncle Tim, I took the back role a lot. I wasn't going to loud talk him, argue with him, or really say anything to defend myself because of the respect I had for him. I just listened. The majority of the time, I never brought up my dad to him or what we may have been disagreeing on at the present time. But this time, I begged to differ. "I'm not apologizing, Uncle Tim. I didn't do anything wrong." "Can't nobody tell me I don't have a right to feel the way I feel; they are my feelings." "I watched my granddaddy go to work in the hot sun every day, killing himself to provide for five other kids that weren't even his responsibility." "My daddy was alive and capable." There was no excuse. I could never see myself putting my girls off on anyone else while I was up and able. Even when I was in the hospital, I wanted them to live there with me so I could take care of them. When they weren't there, I cried until they were in my presence. Being a parent wasn't a choice. Children needed both. In the end, it balanced itself out because of the different qualities they brought. Realistically, neither was capable of covering for the other. Although it was being done every day, a healthy two-parent household outweighed it all.

No matter what I've shown and how much I did for Mari and Zuri, they still wanted their dad present. It became apparent I couldn't do it alone, no matter how comfortable I became with it. Mari was growing rapidly. She was getting older, and boys were now becoming a problem. Her relationship with her father was supposed to be the mold for situations such as these. Interest in boys was inevitable, and I understood that. But the standards started with what her father set. That was either the first person to show you what you deserved or the first one to break your heart.

And it would all be reenacted through your relationships, knowing what you deserved. I taught her that every day. I built her up, and she was confident. But there was still a little uncertainty about her. She needed the reinforcement from her father. He had the ability to make her feel a way I couldn't, like she was the only girl in the world. She loved him more than anything. There was a time he was their hero. But he didn't treat them like that anymore. She needed the protection; she needed to know how to set clear boundaries; she needed to know that settling for less wasn't an option. The way a father made you feel was indescribable. I experienced it a little on different occasions, and when I did, I felt like the luckiest girl in the world. When my dad was present, I felt like I didn't need anyone else. And no one understood me like he did. He was firm and didn't play any games. Anytime I was around him, he spoke life into me and taught me to never conform to the world, even thinking he was better than my grandma because of the love I had for him, just for him to show up one day and vanish the next.

    Fathers really did contribute to healthy emotional development. But instead, I taught her everything I knew and gave her advice on the things I didn't know. We were growing together. My mom isn't present and wasn't much throughout my life. I was just going for it day by day. Sometimes I feel as if I'm doing it all wrong. But I never stop trying to get it right.

    Now that boys were becoming something I had to speak on, I was uneasy about it. It was okay to have a crush, but having a boyfriend was a no for me; she was young and innocent. She also wasn't going to be able to spend any time with him, so there was no point in having one. There was plenty of time for that. She was smart and beautiful. I made sure she was pressure anywhere her foot planted. But she had this arrogance about her I didn't like. I guess that's that Leo shit. When it came to how she handled situations at school with her peers, I loved it. She couldn't be fucked with! She was quiet, so the bullies would try it. But she was checking everything! She wasn't letting shit slide but their asses.

CHAPTER EIGHT

BENEATH THE BANDAGES

My orthopedic surgeon was known to be the best in the county. He was a trauma surgeon and handled most of the cases that came in. While I was occupying the hospital in Georgia, trying to get home, he was the only doctor who accepted my case after I submitted it to several others. Because of my fear of unwrapping my leg, I hadn't seen him in a couple of years. However, my last surgery gave me newfound confidence. He asked me to come in to see what he could do regarding making my leg bend again. He hoped that the blood vessels, tissue, and muscle transferred to my thigh would contribute to more flexion.

"Majic, you look great! How have you been?" he asked.

"I'm so blessed, Dr. Moore; I can't even complain. I've come so far."

"I can't agree more; I've never seen anything like it!" he said. When they told me things like that, it instantly brightened my day.

He asked me to unwrap my leg and get up on the bed. He

closely scrutinized it and quickly came to a conclusion. He said I had an overgrowth of bone in my thigh, along with a large amount of scar tissue that had settled in due to my loss of mobility. He explained that both diagnoses were causing a lot of the stiffness, and he wanted to remove as much as possible. He reassured me that the surgery might not do much considering my situation, which had limited options for correction. Still, it was worth a try. He said he needed to involve Dr. Jessie because there were aspects that only plastic surgery could address. I agreed to it; I trusted them both and knew I was in the best hands.

It was now the day of surgery, and my procedure was scheduled for 7 AM. "Majic Daniels." As my name was called, I stood up and walked to the back. This time, I felt a little better. I wasn't as nervous and scared, but my anxiety was still present. All of the necessary staff came in to prepare me at once. My IV was placed, my blood pressure was taken, they put on my socks, and they asked a ton of questions. The anesthesiologist came in and filled my IV. My eyes fell to my chest, and my body immediately stiffened.

I woke up with my leg and thigh wrapped all the way to my foot, elevated on a device that would keep it bent. There was a knock at the door. It was Dr. Moore. He walked in and explained that everything went well, but most of the scar tissue was embedded and impossible to remove. He had taken out all that could be retrieved. He mentioned that my knee was bending a little more, to about 35 degrees. "It was extremely difficult; we manipulated it as much as possible."

I felt a little discouraged but not surprised. Having just come out of surgery, I figured maybe more progress would happen soon.

Because I didn't have much of a support system, the girls either had to go to Kim's house or Krystal's. I was picky about where they went because I always wanted them to be comfortable. Krystal had a lot going on, but I knew she wouldn't allow my kids any harm. I was waiting to get a response from both of them. Kim called and said she was going to make Steve watch them. I expressed my concerns, and she assured me she would make sure he did what was necessary. After our conversation, I felt secure, as if a weight had been lifted.

Today, when I spoke to the girls, they said they were okay and having fun. They loved their siblings over there. I was now three days in, and Mari was calling to say they hadn't been eating and their dad wasn't there. It became an ongoing daily concern.

I didn't know what was going on or where Kim was, but I was sick to my stomach! She knew how much I stressed about them! There was nothing I could do, and no one I could call. My uncle was always on the go and was never in the area. Ebony was going through a lot and had so much on her plate; plus, she was still grieving from my cousin burning alive in the car accident. Rico had recently started hanging around Steve again and was there most days, but he hadn't been himself lately.

I cried my eyes out every day. Dr. Moore instructed me to stay longer than expected because of all the swelling I was experiencing. I'm talking at least three times the size of my other leg. They took me for X-rays to see if there was any fluid that needed to be drained. But swelling in my leg was nothing new to me. I suffered from it every day because I had undergone so many surgeries that my lymph nodes were not functioning properly. I wanted to call Nick. The thoughts kept coming, but I couldn't bring myself to do it. I knew that when it came to my girls, he would come (BY ANY MEANS)! But I didn't want to need anyone, and I wasn't speaking to him like that.

Before my event, we were doing well—amazing, to be exact! We were going to the stores, buying things, and getting him comfortable in his new home. We spent a lot of time together, eating and hanging out. We became more intimate as well, seeing each other nearly every day.

After the event, while he was reading my book, he kept calling me to apologize. He explained that he never meant to make me feel the way I expressed. Every time we hung up the phone, he would call right back. "Thank you for always being so supportive and loving me. I know at times I don't show it and act like an asshole, but I love you just as much."

"Thank you for not giving up on me. I love you, girl." I responded, "I love you, boy." (That was our little thing.) Soon after, he sent me a text expressing empathy and remorse, explaining the reasons he acted the way he did. He assured me it didn't have anything to do with me. He became vulnerable, and I felt safer. I loved the change that was being made on my behalf. Whenever I expressed that I wasn't feeling well mentally, he came over. If he couldn't make it, he called to comfort me. At those times, that's really all I needed. His presence was my safe space.

Not long after, he tensed up again and became distant. He stopped being open, and his responses took longer than usual. The pain from being ignored felt as intense as physical pain, especially given my abandonment issues. He knew how I felt about that. It was beyond just thinking he was with someone else; it cut me open and made me feel like I had done something wrong. I became anxious, trying to figure out all the things I could have done differently, dissecting our text messages to see exactly what I said. In reality, I hadn't done anything wrong. He pulled away because he felt he was becoming too open. He said things between us were always too intense. I concluded that he wanted to stay emotionally detached, so I ended things with him. Whatever we had, I no longer wanted to participate. I could tell he didn't want it that way, but he didn't understand how he kept hurting me. I knew I hurt him with the message I sent, but I didn't mean any harm. I told him if it was meant for us, divine timing would bring us back together. It was important for me to keep walking away from things because there was a time I stayed in a situation far too long when I knew I deserved better. Choosing myself, no matter how much it hurt, was something I had become accustomed to. Some days I cried; some nights I thought I wouldn't make it to see the next morning, and some days I felt okay. But there was never a day he wasn't on my mind. I counted the days as they passed.

On day 12, he texted saying he wasn't feeling well. I asked why, but he didn't want to talk about it; he just said, "Nothing you need to worry about." I think he just missed me. I wasn't feeling well either; being without him was hard. But I kept it brief. I wasn't trying to get all caught up, and besides, I was now dating someone. We spent a lot of time together, trying to see how far things could go. The night before my surgery, we went out. The guy was incredibly attractive—dark-skinned, very clean, well-groomed, nicely dressed, with a brush cut and a nice full beard. He was draped in jewels, very laid back and chill, but extremely confident and masculine. I was really into his beard. We vibed well every time. His outlook on life and mindset were undeniably attractive; I had a passion for positive thinkers. But at the same time, he didn't mess around at all. I knew all this wishy-washy stuff with Nick would have to come to an end because I didn't want to be the reason for any of Ty's suffering. He often spoke about how he had been wronged because he was a good guy. And as silly as that sounds, it was true. Being a good woman never got me anywhere. When you're a good guy, some women think they've hit the jackpot. We were still getting to know one another, but he showed a lot of concern for me. Allowing him to be there for me at the hospital would have given me solace, but I wasn't sure if this was long-term or temporary yet.

The X-rays came back negative for fluid. I had been in the hospital for a week! Every chance I got, I told them I needed to go home. The next day, they discharged me, but they said I had to go to a rehabilitation facility because of the type of procedure that was done. I could have passed out! Ever since Mari called me, I had been depressed. Soon after discharge, I was transferred to the facility, and all I could do was cry. I didn't eat or interact with anyone. When physical therapy came to my room, I had my head under the covers, pretending to be asleep. Once I told the staff I wasn't coming home, they cried too. I asked them to just give me another week, and I'd be there. I began to wake up earlier than everyone else. I showered, changed my clothes, brushed my teeth, fixed my hair, ate my fruit, and sat in the wheelchair waiting for them to come get me for physical therapy. When they walked in, I was standing up and walking to the bathroom. "We didn't know you could walk!" They had no idea I could fly too when those girls were involved. For the next three days, I beat the sun up. Every day, I told them I couldn't stay there. I had to go. They told me they were about to get my discharge papers ready since I was walking. I asked Uncle Deon to go get my car and bring it to me. As requested, he did. The staff pushed me outside in the wheelchair and kept asking if I was able to drive. Even though I was in pain, I couldn't show any signs of weakness. I rose out of the wheelchair and walked to my car. I couldn't risk another setback of not making it to the girls. I got in my car, turned on Boosie, and headed to get them. I didn't tell them I was coming; I just called when I was downstairs. After pulling in, I got out of the car and waited for them. They ran into my arms, and Mari burst into tears. I thought something else had happened; I thought maybe someone had done something to her. She said they were hungry and that she never wanted to go back there. That situation was pitiful. My only concern was for my kids. I got what belonged to me and got the hell out of there! I went home and cooked them a meal because they loved homemade food. Yes, I was in pain, and they advised me not to stand for long, but that was part of being a mother. No one else was coming to save me or them.

The guy I was dating often offered to help, but it was too soon for him to be around my girls or come to my home. My home is my sanctuary, and my girls are my prize. I was taking him seriously, but I was also taking things slow. The situation with Jason made me uncomfortable opening up like I did before. He was the last guy I allowed myself to get involved with like that. I was still a lover; in fact, I'm an even bigger lover now. But I had to fully observe the situation without involving myself first. I couldn't allow things to take off so fast, even if I wanted them to.

The night before my surgery, about two weeks ago, Nick texted saying he prayed for me the night before and that he knew everything would be okay. He reached out the next day as well to see how things were going. At the time, things were okay. He shared some poetry with me, and honestly, I never knew he could write. There was a time he shared his feelings, but nothing like what I had just heard. He was talking about a girl, referring to her as an angel. I asked if he ever let her hear it, and he said it was just something he wrote, not specifically for anyone. But I couldn't help but think he was talking about me. We already weren't on good terms, and he was showing a more vulnerable side. I doubted he would send me a poem about someone else. In return, I shared something I had been working on.

"*I sucked on the scrotum of his thoughts until he moaned prosperity. I gripped his shoulders from behind and slow ground my fully aroused sound mind against his childhood traumas until tears of healing started to fall. From behind, I put my hand around his throat in the most passionate way and my lips on the tip of his ear. I whispered, 'Strip for me.' He replied in a low tone, 'I'm already naked.' I said, 'No, remove your insecurities, remove your childhood pain, and your confusion. I want to touch you in places no woman has ever touched you. I want you to open your mind for me.' He turned around and stroked my divine knowledge. I gripped him by his head and pulled him backward until his neck was slightly arched, and he moaned, 'I love you.' I replied, 'No,' while thrusting my knowledge into the eroticism of his mind. 'I need you to love you; that's the only true love that will ever matter.' He climaxed, and climaxed again, and climaxed again until he stood up a renewed man.*

My entrance overflowed with the joy of tearing down his ego in a way no woman had ever succeeded. He had only ever fingered the clitoris, never experiencing how being fully aroused could truly satisfy him. But as he went deeper, he was able to penetrate what my pool of moisture really felt like. He knew I was different but had never been able to process the thought of me making love to him without ever even touching him. After he stood up, he turned around with his eyes low, afraid to admit what had just transpired. But I didn't want him to. I wanted to show him I didn't have to use the heart of my femininity to create his happiness. All I had to do was acknowledge his pain and give him a safe place to have an erection. He choked me and turned me around, his manhood slightly thrusting against my ass. I was instantly turned on, but I grabbed his arm in defense because I felt weakened… now the tables had turned. He was in control. He said, 'Strip for me.' I replied, 'I'm already naked.' He said in the most intense way, 'No, remove your masculinity, your ability to be in control, your inner child traumas, and follow my lead.' He put his hand between my legs and entered me. I gasped as I gripped the hand that was choking me while the other scratched his waistline. He said, 'Let go.' I dropped both hands, but he repeated, 'LET GO!' I cried, afraid of losing myself, but he touched me in every place no man had ever known to touch me. My cries became louder as he applied more pressure. My orgasm was so immense that I dropped to the floor, curling up into a corner. As our eyes met, he picked me up and said, 'Thank you; now we're both renewed.'"

"Damn girl, you a freak. You got a nigga all hot and bothered," we both laughed.

"It's all an illusion," I responded.

"Mommy, can we race now?" Every time I had a new surgery, Mari and Zuri wanted to know what they were doing to me next. They knew the seriousness of the situation, but Zuri still had hope because she was younger.

"I'm not sure; we have to see, but if not, it's okay."

"I'll race you on the scooter, okay?"

"Okay," she smiled. She had been asking me to race her for a long time. But I knew that I'd never be able to run again. Even though they always wanted to know things regarding that subject, I kept some information away from them as well. They knew I couldn't run, but it was different to make them worry about me. Mari worried about me a great deal, and even when I told her not to, she couldn't help it. The times she would try to hide it from me, I could still see. Or she'd express it to someone else.

Before I was discharged from the facility, while attending

physical therapy, the therapist told me my knee was bending 25 degrees. It was less than what Dr. Moore said he was able to achieve, but that was while I was under anesthesia. Honestly, it was probably just the force I was able to withstand because I was numb. Either way, it still wasn't doing anything. What was even crazier was that I wasn't even mad. Sometimes I scared myself because I was always able to keep going. It was Monday morning, and time for me to go to my follow-up with Dr. Moore. I struggled to get into the car because I was still sore. I made myself as comfortable as possible and began to drive downtown.

"Majic, how are you feeling?"

"A little pain, but I'm okay," I said.

He continued, "I thought we were going to be able to get more movement out of it than we did. Even under anesthesia, we were only able to get it to 35 degrees with manipulation. I'm sorry, Majic, but there's nothing else I could do."

I became short of breath hearing the words he'd spoken. "I can't give you a knee replacement because I'll have to remove all the hardware from inside your leg. And I'm 90% sure it'll cause blood clots and infection, leaving me to have to amputate your leg. Also, your leg doesn't have the right structure internally for the stability it requires. Even if you did qualify for it, you're too young; it wouldn't last the rest of your life."

There was nothing I could say. All I could do was bawl. Although I knew this, the things he'd just told me hurt to hear.

"Myself and other doctors put in too much work; I won't take a chance risking your life."

"I know it's not easy to hear, Majic, and I know you've heard this many times: trauma patients don't usually survive this. The injuries you've sustained aren't something you see often. Wipe those tears and keep changing the world. We all love you, and if you ever need me, you can come back anytime. Put her in for ongoing future appointments," he demanded of the front desk assistant. I walked to my car in a little more pain than I had come in with. But once I pulled out of the parking lot, it was behind me. The girls were about to go out of town for a couple of weeks, so I had a little free time.

(Phone Rings)

"Good morning, Ty."

"Good morning, beautiful. How was your appointment?"

"Everything went okay," I said.

"Why do you sound like you've been crying? Let's go out," he insisted.

I didn't like discussing it much with him because it irritated him every time. If I was swollen or in pain, he was ready to go find Jason and was adamant about it. He was ready to mess some things up. He didn't understand how a man could put a woman in such a position and just move on as if nothing ever happened. Sometimes, the extent of his anger would upset me. I didn't want to talk about Jason. I didn't care about him and never spoke of it. I felt like he was giving Jason attention he didn't deserve, which is why people never heard me say his name. He would get so mad that it would ruin the rest of his day. I understood because I knew he cared about me, but I would say, "Let's not give him the energy he doesn't deserve." He was dangerous, and I didn't need him getting himself into any trouble. I agreed to meet up with him; besides, I needed a hug. It never failed—each time I graced his presence, his face lit up. He put his arms around me, and I melted into them. His aura was heartwarming. He provided comfort as well as protection. I knew I was safe. I even found myself becoming softer and smiling more. It was different because with most guys I had run into, I talked so much. I could feel who was exactly right for my nervous system. Life had shaken me up so badly, and I had been stuck there ever since. Survival mode was my newfound home, and no matter how many times I tried to pack up and leave, I went right back.

Nick had been reaching out for the past few days. Some days my responses were delayed because I was in his company. His attention was always on me, so it was awkward to continue picking up the phone in front of him. Sometimes I didn't respond at all, and he didn't like it.

"Damn, you got a guy blowing you up," he said.

"I'm sorry; I'll let you know when I'm home," I responded. There was something at my house he needed. My day quickly turned into night, so I never reached back out.

"Hello!", said Nick.

"Good morning, I'm home; you can come," I said.

I opened the door for him, and we began to smile at each other's presence. I gave him his belongings. He asked, "Do you want to get a smoothie?"

"Yes," I responded. I changed my clothes, and we headed for the door. He opened the car door for me and closed it after I was in. While I was in the hospital, I told him I was dating someone and taking him seriously. He said he was happy for me, but I knew he didn't like the times I was with him. And being me, I didn't want to hurt him. But I couldn't wait for Nick forever. I continued dating him, and the more I did, the more Nick showed he cared. The next morning, he texted, "Are you home?" After I replied yes, he instructed me to open the door for him. He was at the door holding a smoothie for both of us.

"Thank you," I smiled. I appreciated all gestures, especially the small ones. We spent the day together watching television and lounging around. As the sunset approached, I walked him to the door. We awkwardly stood there gazing into each other's eyes. He held his arms out for a hug, and I wrapped my arms around his waist. After looking up again, we both lustfully stared at one another and began to kiss.

Damn! I was in love with one guy while dating another. That's why I never tried seriously dating. Every time I was out with someone, Nick never seemed to leave my mind. I didn't want to get anyone involved in that. Besides, I was feeling Ty. I knew he was good for me. He was emotionally intelligent—just what I needed. But I didn't want to overthink it either because something seemed to happen every time I met someone. I started to wonder, "Am I supposed to be alone?"

He bragged about me to his mom every time she called. "Look at her, Mommy! I'm going to bring her to see you," he said as he turned the camera on me while on FaceTime.

Things were going steadily for us. He wanted to start doing more. Our first upcoming trip is in September.

Things started looking crazy for us. He said it was due to legal reasons, which affected our relationship tremendously. During the times we talked, he wasn't in the right mindset. Our conversations were brief, and the situation often had him agitated. He told me not to worry, that there wasn't anything to be worried about, but he was worrying. And the more he worried, the further he pushed me away.

"You're too good for me to allow you to go through this; you've been through enough." He didn't have to tell me that because I wasn't going through it anyway. It was too soon for me to invest myself that deeply. There were so many things I needed that we hadn't even begun to scratch the surface of. But I was just letting it play out. I wasn't even certain if that was truly happening as well. I did have my doubts.

He stopped making time for me, and the time between our conversations spread further apart. Part of me started to question his credibility. At this point, I didn't even want to be a good woman anymore. The situation was tiring.

"Hello," I said, answering Ty's call. I could still hear the smile in his voice through the phone.

"Hey, beautiful! Hey, Mami, I miss you. And guess what else, Mami? Everything's good now; they had nothing on me."

I was conflicted. How did I know he was being truthful about the situation? The way he changed made it difficult to open back up. We continued to date, but the same thing was going on. I wasn't hearing from him as much, and when I spoke on it, he acted like he was always busy.

He seemed trustworthy, and I didn't feel he wanted to cause me harm. But it seemed like more issues were going on. Also, the way he was treating me while under pressure stood out to me. If I'm going to be your significant other, you're going to have to learn to express your anger, even in frustration—not be mean to me and expect me to be understanding. I don't take well to being pushed away. We didn't have history, nor did we have a chance to establish anything stable yet. And because he was pushing me away, I couldn't trust that he would be around. I've met more deserters than fighters. I wasn't completely saying "forget him"; I just needed to observe the situation a little more before I took him seriously. This is someone who says he wants to be around permanently. Do I let my guard down, or am I being naive?

CHAPTER NINE

HEALING WAVES

In the midst of it all, I was drowning in sorrow, still healing from the last surgery and silently suffering alone. As long as I was in someone's company, I was okay; the minute I was alone, the agony hit hard. Being in my head became my home. The pain from my body took hit after hit after hit, silently killing me, and I never said a word. Laying in pitch-black darkness, I hoped someone would shed a little light and rescue me.

I wasn't getting out much because the constant pain was debilitating. As I lay awake, my mind abruptly traveled back to that day—the time I was in the hospital, crying myself to sleep night after night, miles away from my daughters. I had no use of my legs, weight falling off my body but somehow still remaining on my shoulders. Each time I tried to snap out of it, I was yanked back in, unable to escape because I had sunk so deep. I tried to tell myself, "Maj, you're not there anymore," but my body was saying something different: "You can't move," echoed in my ears.

Eventually, that's what I started to believe. But the minute I got up, my heart felt happy, my body felt lighter, and my mind felt free. Nostalgia haunted me, as if it were out to get me. My body said, "Push through," while my mind screamed, "You can't!"

My blood type element was fire-based. I needed to be in the sun a lot to gain energy. The more sun and movement I got, the stronger I became. Fire elements cannot stay indoors or they'll become weakened. As soon as I stepped outside, I felt like I existed, like I mattered. I felt recharged and rejuvenated. Being repeatedly cut off from the world made me feel more alone than I already was.

Contact with Ty wasn't fulfilling anymore. Nick and I were good, but I was scared. I loved him with all my heart, but as soon as I let my guard down, I knew I would end up regretting it. I had lost trust in being vulnerable with him. He was gradually no longer a source of comfort for me. He had always been the only person I felt comfortable being everything with, even intimate. If it wasn't him, I wasn't doing it. It had now been a while, and I didn't care. I truly wanted to experience someone else in every way.

"Where your pretty ass at?" Kirk asked.

"I want you with me!" he demanded.

Kirk had been checking for me since my event. I knew he was interested, but I just couldn't get over how full of himself he was. I usually walked straight past guys who acted like that. I couldn't deny he was also a businessman, a great father, and we often had intellectual conversations. He was very intelligent. Since I had been feeling uneasy, I took that time to get up and get out. I could use the laughs we shared. If only he could keep calm. He kept going on about his looks. I think he just wanted me to see him the way he saw himself.

He asked that I send him my location, but it's rare that I allow people into my home. Instead, I told him I would send it when I made it to my cousin Ebony's house.

I stepped out of the car wearing a brown and black two-piece that slightly revealed my stomach. "Girl, you're so beautiful! I've been messed up about you for so long. You just won't give a guy a chance," he said. He said that every time we interacted, whether in person or over the phone.

We hung out for the remainder of the day until night fell. It became a daily occurrence for him to want me in his presence. I started looking forward to the time we spent together. The more time we spent, the more passionate he became. He was already that type of guy—very outgoing and unreserved. His character and personality reminded me of Kevin Gates, filled with eroticism. Those guys try to talk you out of your clothes. They're manipulators, sweet talkers, and they're not afraid to express themselves sexually.

Sex wasn't something I did often; it was very sacred to me. I held it in high regard. It was an emotional connection, and Nick was the only person I had been attached to in such a way for a long time. I often felt like I was betraying him because that's where my heart lay.

Over time, I began spending entire nights with him. Kirk never wanted anything from me. He never asked me to do a thing; he was solely focused on my every need. Each time we were together, he massaged my legs and feet. I was hesitant when it came to that, but in a way, he made me comfortable. He was never aggressive with me, and he knew the value of my presence.

He gently slid my pants off and gripped my ass, caressing my body as if I were the last woman he would ever encounter.

"Take your bandage off," he spoke softly, but I could tell he meant it.

This guy had lost his mind! I knew he wouldn't judge me, but it wasn't about that. It was a deep wound, and to strip down naked like that—I had never done it in front of a man. Ebony and my friend Andrea were the only ones who had ever seen me that way. My scars and swollen leg were already exposed to him, but this was next-level intimacy.

"Please, Maj, please, I want to massage it," he begged. I continued to deny him, and eventually, he stopped asking. He flipped me over and firmly grabbed my ass. "Girl, when did you get all this?" We both laughed aloud. He slid his legs off the bed and began to pleasure me in every way imaginable. He got up off the bed and sat on the floor while I stood in front of him, my ass facing his face. He pleased me until I climaxed over and over again. In that moment, he asked nothing of me except to embrace my femininity and simply be present. I never even thought about sex.

Dating wasn't easy for me. People assumed that because I was beautiful, it must have been. But it was far from that. Either the person believed I was deceiving them and tried to outmaneuver me, or they accused me outright. In reality, being beautiful made dating even more challenging. It seemed as if people would only lust after me, never truly valuing all that I was. It was more about proving, "I pulled her." It also made jealous and insecure men uncomfortable, to the point that they tried to dim my light. And although I was confident, there was never a moment when I didn't feel the need to speak about my scars because they were impossible to ignore. The significance of the situation affected them too. Most times, people don't like it when you're aware of your power, and fortunately, I was well aware.

I had healed from the inside out, so there was nothing anyone could use against me. I loved myself. I treated myself with the utmost respect. I spoke and acted in a way that represented who I was. So to some, it came off as bougie, stuck-up, or arrogant. Truth be told, I was far from that. But the Most High held me to a higher standard because I was here on a divine assignment.

Knowing your worth will run most people off because there's a certain way they have to show up to be in your life. They've never experienced someone of your caliber, so they treat you as they would treat anyone else, and that's where they lose you. A lot of men haven't done the inner work on themselves, so they project their issues onto you. But I held them accountable. Once they see you're not someone to play with, they often run instead of taking the initiative to heal, just leaving. And although that's a benefit, it hurts. For those who have suffered from abandonment, the part that stings the most is their walking away. You begin to think you weren't worth fighting for. Truly, I'm not toxic or dramatic, but I have triggers. Being abandoned and ignored takes me back to the little girl who felt alone—who was alone. There was no one who understood me. Although my siblings and I shared some of the same experiences, we didn't carry them the same way. My mother's absence weighed heavily on me; I wore it everywhere. It didn't become lighter until my accident happened.

A mother's love is unconditional and undeniable. I know that because that's the way I love my daughters. So if your mother can walk away, hell yes, I have my guard up sometimes. The first thing people will say is, "Heal." But no matter how much you heal, you will always want to know, "Why wasn't I worth staying for?" I get it, but healing comes in waves. I would rather someone let me know what's going on in their life at the present moment that's preventing them from showing up for me than just walking away. But men run from any sign of vulnerability, thinking they will be judged, not considering how it will ease the chaos in their partner's mind.

And one thing about it: I wasn't settling. I could have zero guys on my line, and I still wouldn't settle. If they didn't align with me or we couldn't coexist, they had to get away from me. I had a character and an aura that could make anyone feel better.

I was well-respected. Real men loved me and showed it. I was set apart, and I held that title. It may hurt, but the fact that they walked away because they knew they couldn't show up in the way I needed them to—I respected it. I didn't like it, but I respected it.

Things were complicated in my life, and I took a lot too seriously. I just needed to unwind that night with Kirk. I needed an escape. I wanted to step outside myself and feel different for once. I don't do drugs; I can't handle anything. I needed to feel exactly how he made me feel in that moment. I was living, not just existing. I felt needed. He never stopped bragging about how sexy I was. He cherished me. Although I was very self-aware, I was guarded. So when we were together, he made me embrace it more. No matter if we were getting out of the car or entering an establishment, he was all over me. There was one night we went to the movies, and he stopped to ask one of the staff members to take our pictures. I was being shy because it wasn't that serious to me. I wasn't affectionate, so it felt cringy, but I liked the way he made me feel. It was like I had to step outside of what I was used to. I even started showing my legs more often when we were together. Somehow, I became comfortable never showing them, knowing I could still rock a pair of shorts. It never failed; as soon as he laid eyes on me, he couldn't focus.

The more time I spent with Kirk, the more Nick wanted to talk things out. He eventually told me he didn't want to lose me; he just never had someone love him in the capacity I was able to. Sometimes, he felt undeserving of it. We began working on gaining a better understanding, and the time spent with one another became significant.

"Things feel different this time," he said.

"That's because you're allowing it to happen," I responded. He was absolutely right; things did feel different. We were both happy with how things were playing out, and it showed through our actions.

"Hey, big daddy, do you want to go with me to a poetry event tomorrow night?" I asked.

"Yes," he responded.

"Okay, be ready by eight," I said.

I didn't expect him to want to go to that type of setting, but if he said no, I planned on bringing Kirk. Nick was always my first choice, no matter how much I talked.

I was so nervous, like it was our first time meeting. He still gave me butterflies. I pulled into his parking lot, reversing into a space, waiting for him to get to the car.

I watched as he approached. You couldn't tell me this wasn't the finest guy in the world. He was clean and crisp with a fresh haircut and a nicely trimmed beard. The aroma from his cologne filled the car.

"I love your hair; you look so pretty," he said, looking over at me and smiling. We pulled off and made our way to the venue. My hair was in a blonde bob with brown roots, hand-curled with a side part—looking laid! I stepped out of the car wearing a black two-piece, halter top, and mini skirt, with printed thigh-high boots and a matching purse. I watched him as he watched me make my way out of the car. He was such a stiff guy, so it was intriguing how much I could capture his attention.

Upon entering the club, we were greeted by the host. She complimented me on how beautiful I looked and pointed us in the direction of our reserved seats. We were in the front row. I always had to be accommodated, or I would be uncomfortable the whole night. We took a seat at the bar while waiting for our order. He tipped the bartender before we proceeded to our seats. The show was amazing—nothing but erotic poetry. The ambiance and the drinks definitely made my blood rush. I knew he was enjoying the show; he was thoroughly amused by their level of seduction.

As the show came to an end, we stood up, giving me a chance to stretch my leg and wake my foot. He held my hand as we headed for the front door. My body language screamed intense arousal, and I knew he could tell because I could tell he was feeling the same way. I didn't care, and I wasn't trying to hide it. He then said, "I bet everybody's fucking in their cars right now." We both burst into laughter. I knew if he didn't feel the same, he wouldn't have mentioned something like that.

After we made it back to my house, he helped me pull off my shoes. I let the music play as we undressed each other. Love, passion, affection, and intimacy filled the room until our bodies exploded, making love to one another. He carefully pulled my hair back so he wouldn't mess it up; he said he loved it so much. The amount of attentiveness he showed in that moment made me know our feelings were mutual. His facial expressions while he was stroking me were self-explanatory. I didn't want to get in over my head, but he couldn't hide it forever. He was human; he had feelings too. But the problem was that he didn't want to feel, and I made him feel everything. He had been through a lot that he didn't deserve. But when would he realize he was still worth loving? He was in the company of the purest love he could ever ask for, but he would never allow himself to receive it.

CHAPTER TEN

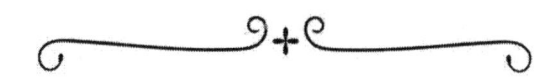

ISSUES OF THE HEART

My grandfather's sister, my aunt, was coming to visit me while I was in the trauma center when she began to fall ill. She struggled with memory loss and had been diagnosed with dementia. Kiara and I were planning a trip to Georgia to visit her within the next two weeks, but she passed away before we could make it. She was the most loving person ever. My mom was her favorite, and she passed that love down to us. During our holiday visits, she would always have at least fifteen different desserts, and her skills were unmatched. Her Key lime cake was my favorite. Whenever I needed prayer, I would call her, or she'd be the one calling me. It was painful because few people truly cared about us.

It was almost time for me to get ready to go out of town. The girls didn't want to come, and I wasn't in the mood to deal with all their complaining. My patience was wearing thin because of the situation at hand. They wanted to stay with Nick, and since he agreed, I let them. He picked them up the night before since we were leaving early the following morning. My mom's sisters, Aunt

Toya and Tracy, Uncle Deon, Kiara, and I packed up the car and headed out for my aunt's funeral.

Both of my grandparents were from up there. Anytime we visited, the hospitality was nothing short of amazing. They loved seeing my mama's kids. As soon as we arrived, we went to my grandma's sister's house. She was standing in the doorway as we pulled in, and more family members were gathered in the yard. We all jumped out, hugging each other. Not many of them had seen me since I was in the trauma center. The last time I saw her, she and about twelve other family members came to visit me. I was in room 502, and I wasn't doing well. I remember her standing in the hallway crying, while my grandma's other sister sat in the chair next to my bed, also crying. "I'm going to be okay, Auntie," I said, even though I didn't believe it. They saw what I was going through, and I just knew I wasn't coming out of there alive. She knew it too; I could see it in her face.

I walked around the car to greet my aunt, and she was stunned!

"Maj, look at you! You look like a baby doll!"

"I can't believe this; you look so good!" And I couldn't agree more; I was beautiful as ever! That made it easy to mask my battles, and because of that, people never truly knew what I was going through.

We all went inside to freshen up. Shortly after, I laid down—I needed some rest.

The next day was her wake, followed by a fish fry at an Airbnb. I was doing my best to reduce some swelling, knowing I'd need all the energy I could muster. Once we got together with our cousins, they'd want to party all night, as usual.

We left my aunt's house and went to one of our cousin's

homes, while Kiara and Uncle Deon stayed with another cousin where the boys were. On the way to the viewing, my stomach was in knots from nervousness. Everything still felt surreal—I hadn't fully come to terms with who we were about to see.

When we arrived, there were many people outside. Most had already entered the church, but Kiara and I stayed back. I wasn't ready, and she hadn't been able to attend another viewing since our granddaddy's. We sat there debating whether to go in, but it wasn't really up for discussion. I went ahead while she stayed behind.

My aunt looked beautiful, just as she always did. She was a pastor and was always dressed impeccably, and that day was no different. Still, it was overwhelming. She wasn't just beautiful on the outside; she was a kind, strong, and loving figure for everyone. It felt impossible to believe she was gone. I thought she'd live forever.

My granddaddy adored his sisters, and my mom was even named after his youngest one. Now, the last of the true family anchors were gone, leaving a void that felt impossible to fill.

Some of the family had already gathered at the Airbnb, and more were on their way. By the time we arrived, it felt like a full-blown family reunion. Both sides of the family, my granddaddy's and my grandma's, were there. Compliments about my beauty and my latest project poured in; everyone wanted to know more.

As night fell, even more cousins showed up, and many were surprised to see me. Kiara and I stood together for a bit before I stepped away briefly to chat with my grandma's brother.

"Man, Kiara, look at Maj!" my cousin smiled.

"I know, cuz! That's crazy! I look at her and can't believe it," my sister agreed.

"A real miracle right there, and that girl is always clean too!"

My sister responded, "Always!"

I walked back while texting Mari; she said they were enjoying themselves. They had just taken a bath, and Nick was in the kitchen cooking dinner. She loved Nick so much, and it brought me solace knowing she was comfortable.

My girls were very picky. They didn't like people or their houses either. It was still hard for me to do a lot of things because they preferred to stay home rather than go with my friends while I was out. If I made plans and wanted them to come, they chose to stay home depending on who I made plans with. They were particular about different energies and their food. They were used to a clean home, me buying them whatever they wanted to eat, or even cooking three-course meals. I spoiled them rotten, but it was only because they deserved it. I didn't have many problems with them, at least for now.

We spent three days straight celebrating with my family, but by then, I had no choice but to elevate my leg. It was becoming harder to walk—the more it swelled, the heavier it felt, and eventually, I started dragging it. I knew it was time to rest.

We returned to my grandma's nephew's house, where I took a shower and laid down. Kiara soon joined me. As we lay there, we started talking about our grandparents. The conversation flowed into the night—we laughed, reminisced, and eventually, the tears came. Life just felt so different now.

Despite the ups and downs in my relationship with my grandmother, she had been the foundation of everything we knew. Things had started to improve between us, and so much healing had taken place. But our time together had been cut far too short.

It's so arrogant for us to think we always have time to get

things right with the ones we love. When they're gone, if they didn't know how you felt, it doesn't even matter anymore. All you can do is cry, but it won't change anything. I wish I could get it right with everyone I love, but sometimes you have to love people from a distance. And if I came to terms with their absence, I was at peace if something happened. Because more than likely, they know how I feel; we just couldn't coexist.

It was time for us to hit the road and head back. I wished we could have stayed longer—my family never wanted us to leave when the time came. Seven and a half hours later, we finally arrived at our destination.

Once I was dropped off at home, I rushed inside to use the restroom, grabbed Nick's gift, and headed right back out the door.

His birthday is tomorrow. I was excited about his gift because I had the merchant print a custom message to go inside. My words could instantly transform a bad day into the best. He often said not to buy him anything, but I had to show my appreciation. I appreciated the changes he's been making for me regarding my feelings. It is so easy to bring up a person's flaws or remind them when they are doing wrong, but I also wanted to acknowledge when he was doing right. The amount of love he has been expressing to my girls and me will never go unnoticed.

I didn't know how much that took out of him, but I knew it couldn't have been easy stepping outside of what he was used to. He was sharing something with us that he often said he didn't have to give. But the fact that he was giving it—that had to count for something.

When I arrived, he had just finished dinner and made cupcakes for dessert. Seeing him in daddy mode was an instant turn-on for me, whether they were my kids or his. Even with his nieces and nephews, he didn't play around. Any kid in his presence was safe.

As the new school year was rolling in, I received a call from him.

"Hello," I answered. "Do you think the girls will like these?" Nick asked through FaceTime.

Mari was going into eighth grade, and Zuri was going into second grade. I shopped for everything they needed and satisfied them with the things they wanted. Kim took them for more uniforms, and Nick bought them both two more pairs of shoes to top it off. School was a big deal to me academically. If they didn't perform well in school, everything was canceled. I wasn't going so hard for nothing.

A few months in, Mari started getting into many altercations. She wasn't the troublemaker type; she was quiet but deadly. She was one of those kids you didn't want to mess with, but they would try her anyway because she was quiet. "Fresh to death" was an understatement. She wasn't seeing anybody. I kept them that way because I felt it was my duty as a mother, on top of her being deserving. I loved the way she carried herself. I admired how the boys couldn't get to her. I talked to her a lot about self-respect and holding herself to a higher standard. I put her on a pedestal in hopes she would treat herself the same.

The boys were coming at her left and right, but I still wasn't allowing boyfriends. Peer pressure began to set in, and the choices she was making became a bigger problem. She was my girl. I was the best parent I knew how to be, but for some reason, I wasn't getting through to her anymore. She wanted to do the things her best friend was doing. I called her mom and told her everything because Mari could no longer be her friend. I felt bad because Mari wasn't social; she didn't have many friends. They did a lot together. I would take them out to eat, to the movies, bowling; they had sleepovers, and when I bought for my girls, I bought for her too. I told her mom it was nothing personal, but this was my life. I took being a parent seriously. That was the only thing I was passionate about, and the only thing I was living for. I did that with passion. No child should have as much free will as her mom allowed her to have. Her dad was active, and I admired that. I'm not saying her mom didn't do all she could, but he didn't make things seem like they were okay. She was punished; her phone was taken away. She would go stay with him for periods of time, and he was on her case. But also, when she did well, he took her on cruises, they vacationed a lot, and he bought her anything she wanted. He taught her value while still exerting his authority.

There was nothing against anyone specifically, but I had to handle this problem before it became something too big. I guess it was too late because eventually, Mari was partaking in activities that made a mockery of herself! The actions I found out she was involved in broke my heart. All I could do was cry. She knew better. There's nothing more to be said because she knows how to carry herself. We talk about this too much. She was trying to fit in, not even realizing she was so much more.

I called Kim and told her what was happening. She asked me to bring Mari over and said she was going to deal with her. I couldn't look at Mari anyway; my mouth was getting reckless. Before she left, her counselor came over for a session. I tried to sit there and listen, but I kept spazzing. My tone was obnoxiously loud, and my words weren't necessarily thought out. But no one could tell me how to handle my pain. I had every right to hurt the way I did because I bleed for this parenting thing!

I took her to Kim's house because she was supposed to be

getting disciplined. This wasn't a time for her to act like she was on vacation, but that's exactly what she was doing. Her attitude was disgusting, and I told her she couldn't come back to my house until she got it together. I still had Zuri to raise, and she was seeing all of this. I couldn't risk making her think that what her sister was doing was right. I'm a private person; I keep a lot to myself and inside my household. I felt defeated, and no one knew. I called Krystal and began to tell her everything. "She doesn't need to be over there; go get her!" "They're not going to do anything but make it worse," Krystal said. And that's exactly what they were doing. I pulled up to Kim's house and saw Mari outside.

"Get in the car!" I yelled. She got in, and we headed to Krystal's house. When I pulled up, Nick was there. I guess my sister called and told him, and he immediately came.

"Hello," I answered. "Why did you come over and get her?" Kim yelled. "I don't like how you brought her over here but then came back to get her so another man can discipline her. He isn't her father! And I don't like how you said she can't come back home either."

"You damn right I said she's not coming back. I told her until she gets her attitude right, she's not coming to my house. She's not my only child! I can't have Zuri around her right now. It's crazy because you know I'll never abandon my kids and how hard I work for them. You're trying to find something that doesn't even exist. And you're right; he's not her father, but when your son doesn't want anything to do with her, he's the one who has to hear that!"

"What type of father tells his daughter what your son just said? He really sat there and told her, 'It's normal; everybody does it; you just have to do it the right way.' She's thirteen years old! Then he proceeds to tell me in front of her, 'Y'all talked back to your grandma; y'all were over there being grown too.' In front of my child? What type of shit is that to say? Because if we're going to talk, let's speak facts! Don't even compare me and the way I raise my girls to my grandma!" My voice began to crack while talking to Steve. "I give these girls a safe space; we have open communication. I listen to them; they're able to express themselves, and if I'm wrong, I apologize. I don't normalize pain and disappointment! My grandma never cared to hear us or about our feelings! And don't sit here making her think that shit is cool and acceptable! I don't give a fuck who's doing it; my child isn't!"

I couldn't believe what I was hearing. How dare he bring up my grandma? He knew what was happening and that I didn't deserve that. But more so, I was hearing a father justifying his daughter's actions. That guy had fallen off so badly that he didn't even know right from wrong anymore. He hadn't provided for them in so long that he was just doing anything to get on her good side and make her feel like he was the best parent. Nick would have never told Mari anything like that. She was too embarrassed to even look at him, but in her father's presence, she felt proud. That tells you right there who the real joke was. They were all a joke at this point!

She saw the way they were justifying her behavior, which made her want to be with them even more. I was killing myself, stressing out daily trying to keep her home. But the more I tried to keep her away, the more she wanted to be there. I confiscated everything; she had no means of communication. I left the house to go ship books, which I was only gone for about 30 minutes. Before I could make it inside, Zuri met me at the car.

"Mommy, Mari called Grandma to come get her, and

Grandma told her to pack a bag." I couldn't understand how Kim was grown as hell, upholding the bullshit. She was about to come get my child without my permission, knowing Mari was in the wrong. I decided not to fight it anymore. I told her I didn't want Kim coming to my house; I would take Mari myself. She began to pack a bag. "No, let them provide," I angrily yelled. She wasn't taking a motherfucking thing out of here. I was hurt. I didn't recognize my own child. I went without so they could have all that they wanted. Emotionally, their pain was mine. I wasn't letting anybody play with them. But she knew how I was coming! I was falling out with the world about them. She knew all she had to do was tell me something, and I would handle it, whether it was something positive or negative. All those nice things I bought them were because I wanted them to have it. But now it was their turn. It was Steve's turn to show her what he was all about.

"You're not taking anything out of here. If you need something, let them buy it! The things you need are no longer my problem." It was time for her to learn.

I dropped her off at Kim's house and kept it moving. But I was dying inside. Zuri cried every day, and I cried for Zuri. We had always been inseparable. It had been the three of us for as long as I could remember. I took Zuri out every day to keep her busy. I tried to keep her mind off of it, but every day she asked for Mari. Nick checked on me daily. We'd go get something to eat or just go out to keep me occupied. But when night fell, my pillow caught my tears. Mari started to call to talk to her sister. Listening to their conversations was hurtful. "Sister, are you coming home?" Zuri cried. But Mari's answer would be no. I had to hide my tears from Zuri because I needed to control the situation. "It's okay, Zuri. She's just going through something right now; she'll be home soon." But in all actuality, I didn't have the answers.

About a week later, Mari texted me saying she needed clothes, but I told her she wasn't getting anything from my house. She was their problem now. She said she was going to school any kind of way and that her hair needed to be done. I stopped responding. She told her counselor, and her counselor called. But I didn't let up. If that was where she was going to be, it was time they got used to it. I wasn't sending a motherfucking thing. Did he help out with anything when they needed it? That guy wouldn't even buy a sock for them over here. How I felt? Fuck all of them! Get it how you live, bitch-ass nigga!

"Mommy, I miss you and my sister," Mari texted. I didn't respond. It hurt me, but I needed her to feel every ounce of pain so she wouldn't choose to go through this again. A couple of days later, she texted, "Mommy, I don't have a way to school. I've missed a lot of days because they say it's too far. Can you come get me to take me to school?" This little girl had me messed up! I wasn't doing shit. Until she got her act together, she could forget about me. She texted again and said Steve's girlfriend had bought a new car, but they were still saying they couldn't take her to school. Things were going badly for her over there. They were making every excuse, but there were no excuses when you were a parent. At least on my end, there were none.

She called me and said, "I'm sorry, Mommy. I'm ready to come home. My attitude is better, and I'm sorry for acting that way. Can you please come and get me?" "Sure, I can." I pulled up to get her; she came over to my door, hugged me tight, and began to cry. She got in the car, and we left.

CHAPTER ELEVEN

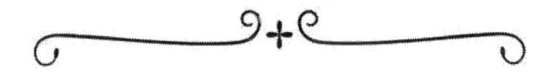

EVALUATION

I found myself bracing for surgery yet again. This time, the plan was to transfer tissue and muscle from the left side of my back to the area at the top of my thigh, just below the base of my buttocks, which had been damaged by the guardrail. It was essential to use an area rich in blood vessels, so Dr. Jessie decided to make the incision along the back of my thigh, extending down toward my calf, to ensure the connection was successful. The girls stayed with one of my best friends, Monique. We had been friends since ninth grade, and her family loved the girls and me as if we were their own. Many days, either she or her mom kept the girls when I needed them to. It never mattered what I needed, even if it was a bill paid. Just like Keyshia and her mom, they didn't want to hear about me and my girls!

Surgery was hard on me this time. I didn't go in with the best spirits; my mind was preoccupied, and I was exhausted. I was ready to be sedated just to enter a state of repose. Directly after exiting surgery, it felt as if a car had fallen on top of me. I was aching, stinging, and throbbing. All I could do was sob. The incision on my back left me unable to move my shoulder as well as my arm. The cut went from the left side of my back all the way across, leaving about an inch of free space that kept it from taking up its entirety. The pain medication continued to knock me out each time I tried to awaken, and it was only then that I realized I was in the ICU. What could have gone wrong? I worried!

While Kiara was visiting, she noticed a large lump that had accumulated on my back. She called the nurse in immediately. After the nurse examined it, she decided to page the doctor. Kiara and I looked at one another and began to worry. This whole ordeal was full of ups and downs, but I couldn't lose sight when things went wrong. There was still a long journey ahead of me, and I wasn't able to determine the outcome just yet. The only thing I knew to do in a moment of defeat was pray. I knew the Most High didn't bring me this far to drop me off in the middle of nowhere. I was in a place of unfamiliarity, and the only way to get out of the unknown was to keep going.

Dr. Jessie entered my room with a smile that lit up the whole floor. Seeing him forced a smile out of me. He walked over to the other side of the bed where my back was exposed. "We're going into surgery in the morning," he ordered. I still didn't know what it was or what was going on, but if he didn't seem bothered, there was no reason for me to panic. I knew I was going to be okay. I trusted him. I could testify that his judgment was certain.

The next morning, I went in for surgery. They removed the excess fluid that had collected under my skin. The surgery went well, but I felt defeated. The weather was sunny outside, but everything around me felt dark. Kiara visited every other day.

Before she walked in, I put on a brave face, and she couldn't tell a thing.

Andrea was a good friend of mine since middle school. Back then, we both visited each other's homes often. The last time I saw her, she unexpectedly dropped by my grandparents' house. I was pregnant with Mari, and we were catching up. Not long after, we lost contact when the house went into foreclosure. Recently, she began to see my work online and reached out to me for a purchase. Ever since that day, it was as if we picked up where we left off. Since I got out of surgery, she's been reaching out, encouraging me to stay positive. We matched each other's energy, for real. She always had the right words to say: "Drea, I can't do this shit. I cried." "You're the strongest person I know; you were made for this. The way you embody this, I'm so proud to call you my friend." "You can't be messed with at all, friend!" she constantly says. This was one of my toughest stays yet, and she tried to keep me uplifted the whole time.

After being transferred to a regular room, I was discharged about two days later. Kiara picked me up from the hospital and then dropped me off at home. When we arrived, she helped me into bed. I was in so much pain that it made me overly emotional. So overwhelmed, I started to cry until it was hard to breathe. In that moment, I felt weak and vulnerable. I didn't like being down like this. The minute I couldn't do for myself, I would rather let it all go. She reassured me that everything was going to be okay. I was hearing what she was saying, but I didn't believe it.

My brain wasn't functioning the same. Each time I was cut, it brought more trauma. Over time, I accumulated a serious case of post-traumatic stress disorder.

"I love you, I'll be back," Kiara said, kissing my forehead. I knew once she stepped outside to leave, she was going to cry. She couldn't handle much mentally anymore either. We hadn't been dealt the best hand. As soon as she left, I cried as I rocked myself back and forth until I was sound asleep.

I answered the phone, and Uncle Tim's voice was on the other end. "Hey, sweetheart," he said sadly. I was a little concerned because if you know my uncle, each time he called me, he was excited. Hearing my voice lit him up. His personality was joyful, so an eyebrow definitely should have been raised.

"What's wrong, Uncle Tim?"

"Your aunt has passed, sweetheart."

My aunt was his and my dad's older sister. She'd been sick for a while with diabetes. It took one of her legs and her other foot before she succumbed to it. I talked to my aunt a lot on the phone and would stop by to visit sometimes. She was tough! Even in her sickness, she wasn't to be played with. She was the biggest shit-talker I've ever known, besides my granddaddy. She rode motorcycles and was part of a motorcycle club. That right there should tell you how tough she was. My dad was her caretaker, so I knew it must have had a great effect on him.

He and I were still on no speaking terms. In all honesty, I wasn't waiting for him to call, but under these circumstances, I thought I'd be the bigger person. He didn't live far from me, so I decided to drive over.

Initially, I knocked, and his girlfriend greeted me at the door. "Maj, it's nice to see you! You look so good!" she said. I gave her a hug as I entered her home. When I walked in, he was in the kitchen sitting on a bar stool. As I began to approach him, he stood up to greet me, and we hugged one another.

"Are you okay? Do you need anything?" I asked.

He was going through some of my aunt's papers and said that he would need my help. I told him I was going into surgery in the morning, but it was a procedure that didn't require me to be cut, and it was outpatient, so I was hoping to be up and going soon after. We agreed to stay in touch.

I briefly stopped by before picking Kiara up; I couldn't stay long. He walked me to my car and expressed some of the things he wanted me to take care of. To start with, he asked if I would design my aunt's shirts and send out the memo to loved ones. I agreed and told him we'd speak more on it after my surgery.

This time, they were taking from my right thigh and transferring it to the left. I picked up Kiara that morning so she could drop me off. I wasn't too scared since it was minor, but there was a bit of anxiety going on. The night before, I dreamed of my grandma. The dream was so detailed and vivid. I often dreamed, and there was always a message behind it. My dreams were a source of reality. Since the accident, I had gained more access to the spiritual realm. I tried not to think about it, but I couldn't help it. I began contemplating going into surgery. Kiara was more scared for me than I was. "Girl, you just go do what you gotta do; don't even worry," she said. Little did she know, I did worry. I just couldn't let it get the best of me. My girls depended on me. No sign of fear could be shown, because then they would worry. It was necessary for me to make them as comfortable as possible.

My doctor was the best in his profession, so even when my anxiety levels were high, I knew he was going to extreme measures to save my life. I was now part of the vanguard family; I knew I was safe.

Dr. Jessie walked into my room to mark the places they would be working on. He gave me a pep talk and was ready to get to work.

"You should've seen it before I started; it looked like an apple core," he told the nurses in the room. He scrolled through his phone and began to show them pictures. He was funny and had no filter whatsoever. They stared at me in complete disbelief. "Wooooowwww, girl, you are blessed!" He had every right to brag because the time and effort he put into my situation was worth taking credit for.

Another surgery was safely completed. I often watched how people went into surgery and never came out, whether it was due to anesthesia or other complications. It shed light on how strong I was physically. I had been here many times and had come out safe every time. It also showed how strong my heart was and how much it could take. Literally speaking, I could handle anything; whether I wanted to or not, I was coming out stronger. There were things that meant the world to me, but I wouldn't trip over them. I'd give myself time to feel it for a little while, but then I'd move forward. I still felt how I felt about the person, but the way I was able to maneuver in my everyday life regardless of it amazed me. For those reasons, I deserved more grace than what I gave myself.

Surgery was successful, and I was back home. I reached out to my dad to let him know I would be there soon to handle the things he needed me to. My legs were bruised, and there was a bit of soreness, but it was nothing I couldn't handle. It was very minor compared to everything else I had been through.

Once I arrived, we started going over the things that needed to be done, putting them in place. I designed the shirts on my phone and sent them out to family and friends, showing them what they could expect. Once they started sending their money, I went to the swap shop to have them made.

Walking was a little more difficult for me today. On top of the discomfort I was feeling, I was also tired. However, I never wanted to let people down, especially if I had said I would do something. I know that's a trauma response—showing up for people in a way you wished they would show up for you, not wanting them to feel an ounce of what you have. It's not just in this situation; I often tire myself out for others, sometimes giving my last, but they'll never know, and I'll never say a word. There are times when I don't know how I will make it through because I do fall short, but I keep silent. Now, I habitually think that if I need help, I'm weak. I've come to believe that strength is defined by how much pain I can endure. But really, a woman was never meant to be strong. As the world changed, roles shifted. They didn't really change, but both men and women stopped doing the things that naturally define us. Women are supposed to be soft, vulnerable, submissive, loving, gentle, and caring, yet today, those qualities are seen as weaknesses. Similarly, men being protectors, providers, logical, and dominant are often viewed as doing something wrong or being "simps." But that's just the way we're structured. I hear people say, "Times have changed," which is true, but the roles of male and female will always remain the same.

I found myself taking on both the roles of a man and a woman in my household. With my daughters, I had to be versatile—sometimes providing emotional support and other times offering logical guidance. However, because everything was coming from me, it often became difficult to distinguish my true self and understand the role I was meant to play.

As I made it to the car, my leg and foot were swollen, and I was relieved to finally be sitting down. I headed back to my dad's house with some shirts. My dad was in charge of everything, and not having much to work with, I stepped in as much as I could. Anything he asked of me, I did, and I was proud that I could help him in his time of need. I could tell he was grateful; many times, he expressed his appreciation. I was surprised because I had never seen him so emotional.

As I was walking into the gas station, I received a call from him. He was in tears on the other end. "Baby, I just want to tell you I love you. Do you hear me? Don't ever think for a second that I don't love you. I love you so much, and I always will. Thank you for everything," he cried.

"I love you too, Dad," I said, hanging up the phone. I felt bad for him because I knew he was grieving, and I seemed to be all he had. I also knew he was apologizing to me for everything I expressed in my book. This was our first interaction since then—at least, that's what I thought he was apologizing for. I assisted him with everything he asked of me regarding my aunt, and not once did I mind. There was so much going on, and the people who had him messed up had me messed up as well. Uncle Tim came down to help us get things situated. When I walked inside the viewing to see her, she looked beautiful—absolutely amazing. All the stress he had endured paid off. He approached me and said, "We did it, baby! She looks good, doesn't she?" And she truly did!

Kiara was outside; she came with me to support. My dad's side of the family was like her family as well. She has more memories with him and my mom than I do.

After the viewing, we went to the park for a fish fry. But when those Royal Palm OG's get together, they don't hold back. We stayed out there all night. My body was feeling it, though. I was in pain. I told Kiara we needed to leave. I knew it wasn't healthy to keep going like I did, but I didn't know how to turn it off.

As I pulled into my sister's yard to drop her and my niece off, Rico approached the car. All of his hair was gone. He had recently grown it out and was excited about the length, so I couldn't understand why he cut it. But he was strung out on drugs, so I doubted he knew what his actions entailed. The streets had him by the throat. Every time he cut his hair, it wasn't a good sign. I was upset with him, so I kept our conversation brief—not just because he cut his hair, but because of the way he was living. This time, it wasn't for fun; he was like a junkie, and it broke my heart because he couldn't shake it. He was like the son I never had.

He would cry out to my sister, telling her how he wanted to get clean but couldn't. I watched him deteriorate right before my eyes, and there was nothing I could do about it. He respected me and listened to whatever I said, but he was too far gone. That demon had a hold on him, pulling him in deeper and deeper. I told him, "Do you think the devil wants someone who's empty inside? No! He wants you because you're full of greatness!"

Rico is incredibly smart—many people don't realize it. I'm talking about an IQ of 160. I always tell him, "You're not meant to be what you're trying to be! Have the courage to step aside and do something the world isn't doing; you've got it, my nigga!" I loved feeding him that encouragement because it fueled his energy. But this time, it seemed like there was no coming back for my nephew. It was necessary for me to disconnect because I'm highly sensitive now, but I dealt with it alone.

After my aunt's funeral and everything was over, my dad and I started talking consistently. Over the next couple of weeks, I would cook and invite him over. One morning, I received a message that was totally unexpected.

"Good morning. First and foremost, I love you and always have, and I always will. However, my reality and story will remain the same, no matter what anyone else thinks. I've always done my own thing and don't need anyone to dance to my music; I've always done the two-step, and I don't apologize for anything that has happened to people indirectly. In this life, things happen.

For the record, I didn't put your mom on drugs or crack. Your mom was getting high with Felicia when I met her, and she started doing crack with Audrey's boyfriend. That's my truth and my reality, no matter what anyone else thinks. If you need someone to blame for your mom's actions and bad decisions, then you need to go to God and ask Him to help you with that, because I will not carry the weight and burden of someone else's actions on my shoulders. Everyone has to own up to their own misfortunes, whether in this life or the afterlife.

I just want to shine a light in your darkness, and if anyone knows the truth, God does. That's what I'm standing on—God's truth."

It's been over a year since my book was released, which is when we last spoke. He's just now addressing it because that has been eating at him. For me, it was how he relayed the message following what he said. Although both were bothersome, coming at me that way wasn't going to solve anything because he really had me messed up. Why didn't you have that same energy when you were crying and wanted my help?

I responded:

"I don't need anyone to blame, and I don't have any darkness. I dealt with everything long before I put my book out; that's why I was able to talk about it openly. I'm the happiest and most grateful person because I know what it's like to not have my parents but still come out on top. I conquered what people thought I wouldn't, all because of what my mama was. I wasn't there to see who gave her her first rock, but everybody else was. You say her actions were bad decisions, and you don't apologize for anything that happened to people indirectly, as if she wasn't a person you were with for many years who had a big influence on her. My mama told you to your face that you got her addicted, and for you to just now address this after my book has been out for over a year means you've been living with it. You've never been able to apologize for anything or take accountability, so I don't expect you to now. But how this message you sent me came off, I'd rather never be in your life. It's been over a year since we talked, and you still never cared to see how I felt or if I needed to be consoled. You lack empathy for your own child while saying you love me. If you did, you would have never delivered this message the way you did—full of arrogance and without a care in the world. Be safe. 🙏"

He responded:

"You're really stuck on stupid, and you're right; I don't have sympathy or empathy for some shit I will not take the blame for. 💚 Likewise."

That guy had some nerve! Referring to my mama like she was a junkie and not someone he was with for many years. Like he wasn't genuinely messed up about her. Talking about her as if she never stood on her own!

If you didn't get her on it, why not help her get off instead of beating her when she didn't want to buy any? My daddy has always been strong as hell—real headstrong. He was able to shake anything off, but not everyone can. After getting her on it, he talks about her as if it wasn't that way. He better put some respect on that! Like I've said, "Yeah, she probably was on coke; it was recreational in the '80s—who wasn't?" But when it came to crack, he was already on it.

I felt used. I couldn't believe he addressed me that way. I'm washing my hands of him! He seems not to care that I'm navigating this world without any guidance, strictly alone! And I have been since I was a teen. If he's saying it's not his fault, why not still take better care? I'm your only child. Don't you think your daughter has lacked enough? Don't you think I need you?

The pain is extensive. It's never-ending! My mama is never coming back, and it's not okay! I am not okay! I'm out here trying to figure this out, trying to be the best mother I can while healing my inner child, digging deep to understand why I am the way I am!

I read something once that said, "I didn't have the emotional or physical connection of any parent. I was a stranger to love. I was a stranger to communication. I was starved of hugs. I was starved of their presence. I grew to learn that love is transactional. I grew to learn that communication is a flaw. I grew to learn that hugs are uncomfortable. I grew to learn that their absence carved a void I would be craving until I take my last breath."

And that's what was happening; their absence has created a void so massive that it's causing me to continuously chase something that I don't even know exists. I just want to feel something. I want to feel alive; I want to be loved so much that it heals me in every way I've ever been hurt. It's possible because I exist.

I'm starved for authenticity, and I'm dehydrated from waiting—waiting on my dad to come and save me. And it hurts to finally realize he's not.

I often wonder how parents could cause so much pain. Over time, I've come to realize that God had a plan; He needed vessels to bring me into this world. My parents were those vessels because I have a purpose; I was chosen. My mother carried me as far as she could, and when her role ended, God took over. My father was never fully present in my life, but he did what he could, as far as he could, until God stepped in. I was never truly theirs to begin with. God needed me to come through brokenness, to experience what was necessary for me to fulfill my purpose.

I honor my father, even in the pain, but honoring him doesn't mean forcing a relationship. I've reached a place of acceptance. I feel no shame or embarrassment because God has always been the father I needed, never leaving my side. My purpose in this life is far greater than what my parents could provide.

A couple of months passed, and here I was facing another surgery—this time on my knee. The procedure was long. By the time I came out of recovery, it was dark. The pain hit me, forcing me to open my eyes! I felt debilitated. A nurse rushed to my side, saying, "I'm going to get you something for your pain now." But the type of pain I was really in, there was no help for it, little did she know. As I cried out, there was a staff member standing behind the desk watching me. My curtains were open, so I was able to see directly behind their station. "What the hell is this woman looking at?" I said to myself. I watched as she approached me. She stood to my right side and began to speak…

"What's your mom's name?" she asked.

"My mom isn't around."

"Do you feel comfortable telling me her name?"

I replied, "Debra," while still crying, and before I could utter the rest of her name, she screamed in disbelief! "Oh my gosh! I knew you had to be her daughter! You look identical to her; you're beautiful! I can't believe this!" she exclaimed.

She grabbed me tightly and hugged me. "Your mom and I were best friends. That was a real one right there," she bragged. "Everyone loved her! Girl, your mama was a bad bitch! When I saw your face, I was in shock!"

It then hit me that if I ever had any doubts before today about the possibility of my mom being alive, this was just confirmation that she wasn't. I'm lying here going through some of the worst pain in my life, and my mom sent an angel to comfort me.

"This is my niece; please bring her meds; she needs them!" They ran over and injected my IV. My cries surrendered, and my head felt heavier, forcing me to drop it, no longer able to hold it up.

"We're waiting on your room to get ready; I'll be right back," she said. Once my room became available, she transported me upstairs. After exiting the elevator and entering the fifth floor, all you could hear was, "Hey, Magic! Welcome back, girl! How are you doing, Magic? Did she show you her book?" a nurse asked my mom's friend.

"You didn't tell me you wrote a book!" I told her I wasn't feeling well and to come back tomorrow, and I would show her; she agreed.

Early the next morning, there was a knock on my room door. It was my mom's friend.

"How are you feeling this morning?" she asked.

"Much better than yesterday," I replied.

Tears formed in her eyes. "My daughter died in a car accident a few years ago, so this is really personal to me. I wish she was still here fighting like you are."

It was just so ironic to me how her daughter died from an accident, and she was one of my mom's closest friends. She was the only one here comforting me at the moment. We were currently healing through one another.

"Let me call my brother and tell him who I'm with right now," she said.

(Phone rings) Vanessa: "Bro, guess who I'm with? You remember Debra?"

Her brother: "You know I remember Debra."

Vanessa: "I'm in front of her daughter right now; she's in the hospital."

Her brother: "Girl, you had a fine-ass mama; that was my baby. I was supposed to be your daddy." (We all laughed.) He told me to get better soon and that he was going to keep my mom in his prayers.

"How's your dad?" Ms. Vanessa asked.

"I don't know; we don't speak," I responded nonchalantly. "There was a disagreement between him and me about my mom and how she got on drugs." He said it wasn't him. Even before all of this, my family spoke on it often.

"It was him! I don't know why he's lying to you. He got her on crack! That was a nasty guy too. He did her wrong," said Vanessa. "I believe she still would've been here if it wasn't for him," she said. It didn't make me feel any different than I was already feeling; I knew what it was.

CHAPTER TWELVE

SHADOW WORK

After being discharged, I was due for a post-operative evaluation in a week's time. My knee was looking smaller, and my ankle wasn't swelling anymore. Dr. Jessie watched me get out of my seat. "I'm going to call a really good friend of mine; he's an awesome orthopedic surgeon. He's younger, and maybe he has some new techniques. Let's try to get you in there and see what he can do for that knee," he said.

I entered my assigned room and put on the gown. I could hear him on the phone from across the room: "Hey buddy, I have this patient; she's awesome. Very young and has been through a lot. I'm currently about five surgeries in. I was wondering what you can do for her? She was in a terrible motor vehicle accident up in Georgia and barely made it out. Her leg sustained a great amount of trauma, and there's extensive damage. I'm trying to get her some kind of movement in it. It's basically a peg leg. You should have seen it before; oh my gosh, it looked like the core of an apple."

He responded, "Okay, send her to get CT scans, and tell her to bring them in to me on a CD. My staff is going to call her to schedule an appointment."

I had never been open to going to another orthopedic surgeon. I had even been recommended to go to a level 2 trauma hospital with great reviews, but I didn't want to take the chance on people who didn't know me. If my orthopedic surgeon said nothing else could be done, I trusted that. I knew he wanted the best for me, but so did Dr. Jessie.

I followed Dr. Jessie's instructions and went to get my tests done and scheduled with the new orthopedic surgeon. I didn't allow myself to get too excited, but I was hopeful. I pulled into the parking lot, cluelessly entering the building and looking for the address. When I found it, I was instructed to fill out paperwork and hand over my CD. I waited as they looked it over, then my name was called.

"MAJIC DANIELS!"

I stood up and followed a guy to my designated room. "The doctor will be in shortly," he said.

The doctor took about 30 minutes to come in. My immediate thought was that there wasn't much he could do for me.

He knocked before entering. "Majic, it's so nice to meet you! I've heard so many great things about you. If I had to say anything, I'd definitely say you don't look like what you've been through."

"Thank you," I responded.

I swallowed hard as he sat down. "Well, Majic, I've never, in all my years of practice, seen anyone survive with your injuries. After looking at your scans, there's nothing I can do for you. You don't qualify for a knee replacement because your leg doesn't have what's needed. You also have accumulated a large amount of scar tissue, which has caused the majority of the stiffness. I can go inside your thigh and remove some scar tissue to give you a little more mobility, but there are no promises. Now that so much scar tissue has grown, it's harder to access, and a major artery is right there, so I have to be very careful while working around it. I just don't think it's worth the risk because you might not gain any more function than you have now, and you're risking losing your leg or your life."

I totally understood, but it was always hard to hear. My eyes watered as I held back tears. "You're a miracle. Each doctor I spoke to on your behalf said nothing but wonderful things about you. Continue being awesome and tell your story because you indeed have a story to tell. I've never seen anything like this. You look amazing; there's no need to cry. Dry your eyes and continue being great," he said.

I took a deep breath and dried my eyes.

I wiped my tears before walking into the house, but one thing about those girls was that they always stayed in my business. Mari would pick up on my energy, so I had to get it together. "What did the doctor say, Mommy?" she asked.

"There's nothing they can do for me," I cried.

"It's okay, Mommy; you still do everything," she reassured me.

Not once had I ever been ungrateful, but it's a wound I thought I had healed from. Every time I ran into a situation like this, it reminded me of how bad my leg really was. Honestly, people didn't know that because I continued on with my life and never complained.

After Mari said that, I didn't shed another tear because she was right. There wasn't much I couldn't do, and for the things I couldn't do, I could with assistance. I never had a problem with anyone helping me.

After that, I decided to seek therapy. I was hurting all around. I felt myself crashing with nowhere to turn, so I shut down from the world. Every time I went missing, Andrea knew what was going on. She would send me messages of reassurance. Even in my times of suffering, she thought I was that girl.

My birthday was rapidly approaching, and I wasn't well. But I was determined to get there.

I began my first therapy session.

As I pulled into the parking lot, my therapist was already outside, waiting to greet me. She approached my car with a warm smile and introduced herself, saying, "Hi, I'm Ms. Michelle, your therapist. It's so nice to meet you."

"The pleasure is mine," I replied, following her inside as she led the way.

We entered a room and sat down at a large round table, facing each other. Before leaving home, I had promised myself I would walk in there, break down, and pour my heart out, ready to share everything. I thought I was fully prepared. But as I began to recount my life, hearing my own voice tell my story, I was caught off guard. I stunned myself.

"Hold up now, your girl is really raw out here. You're in a league of your own!" I said to myself. That realization made me sit straight up in my chair and adjust my crown. It gave me strength and the fight to carry on. No tears were shed—at least not then.

"Majic, you mentioned your grandparents both dying. Can you elaborate?" she asked.

"Yes, of course. My grandmother battled breast cancer for

nearly half her life before it eventually spread to her ovaries. She endured so much. Before that second diagnosis, she had already tested positive and undergone a partial mastectomy. After the cancer returned, my sister Krystal and I became her caregivers as her condition worsened. Over time, it became harder, and Kiara moved back to help us.

When her health declined to the point where she could no longer stay with us, she went to live with Aunt Tracy. This left my siblings and me living in our grandparents' home. However, with my grandmother gone, my aunt wanted us out of the house as well. Things took a turn for the worse—they'd come by and turn off the air conditioner and even try to have the electricity disconnected.

The house was always our home. Our grandparents never denied us a place to stay; we were always considered theirs, even when I moved in with Kim.

During that time, my siblings and I only had each other, and no matter the odds, we stuck together.

I was heavily pregnant with Mari at the time, but we stayed ready for anything—that was just our mindset. Kiara would lead, I'd back her up, and then came Jr. It was a tough time, but we had no one else to stand up for us.

"Yes, of course—my grandmother battled..."

"My granddaddy..." I burst into tears before I could begin. I couldn't get it together.

I continued, "My granddaddy was a special man; both he and my grandmother did a lot to help those in need, and the world could vouch for him.

My Aunt Tracy's husband was very troubled. He used drugs often and would come home fighting with my aunt a lot. Most times, as soon as he got paid, he messed up the money, causing my granddaddy to step in.

One particular Thursday, they were all at my cousin's house having a few beers after getting off work. Her husband worked for my granddaddy's construction business and wanted his check early. After refusing him, they began to tussle. Following my aunt's husband, he picked up a shovel and hit my granddaddy in the head with it."

My voice cracked, and my eyes watered as I spoke. My cries became deafening. That memory tore me up. We never talked much about it, even though it devastated us. I collected myself and picked up where I left off. "I remember the house phone ringing while I was changing my niece's diaper, Kiara's second child. It was my cousin on the other end, saying to get there because something happened to Granddaddy. My grandma dropped the phone and screamed, 'Something happened to Dennis! Come on, y'all!'

I remember snatching my niece off the couch while we all ran to the car. When we pulled up, my grandma barely put the car in park before she got out. Destiny and I jumped out of the car behind her, seeing my granddaddy sitting on the back of the truck, swaying his head from side to side. His head was bleeding while he seemed to be in a daze.

We lost it! I felt hopeless! I remember jumping up and down on the sidewalk, holding my stomach and screaming, while falling to the ground, not knowing what to do. I called Kiara; she was still away at school. But I was crying so hard she couldn't understand me.

I calmed down and started to tell her, "Robert hit Granddaddy in the head! Granddaddy is bleeding and not talking!"

Kiara began screaming on the phone, causing us to be disconnected. As I was on the phone with her, Uncle Deon pulled up the same way my grandma did, jumping out before even putting the car in park.

"Nigga, you hit my daddy! You did this to my daddy!" he shouted while approaching Robert. "No, no, that's not what happened," but my uncle wasn't trying to hear that. We all knew Robert, so there was nothing believable he could have said. Uncle Deon got in the back of the ambulance with my granddaddy as they left for the hospital.

Destiny was taking it just as hard as I was because she lived with us. Robert is her dad, but she always despised him. Her relationship with my granddaddy was as close as mine. They played around all day.

"When my granddaddy got to the hospital, he was rushed to ICU. He wasn't doing anything pertaining to functioning on his own."

Kiara and Aunt Toya were on the next thing smoking, coming from Daytona. After they made it home, we all went to see him. I remember us being in the elevator in silence. Once we got off the elevator and walked through the double doors to the department he was in, his room was the first one on the left. We saw him and couldn't contain ourselves. He was hooked up to machines with tubes all over him, unresponsive. Thinking about it, he was just like I was.

The doctor said there was bleeding on his brain and that they also saw a spot on his brain that looked to be cancer. They had to get us up out of there! A few weeks prior, Kiara went to the doctor with Granddaddy to see if the cancer had returned to his lungs. However, she had to be back at school before the results came in.

When she called Granddaddy to ask about the results, he told her everything was negative and that there was nothing to worry about. But now, we believe he wasn't telling the truth. The cancerous spot that was now showing on his brain resulted from cancer in his lungs. Because there was an open wound, it spread to his brain.

He stayed in the hospital for about a month. By the time he came home, he was no longer the Granddaddy we remembered. His hair was gone, he was already skinny, but now he was even skinnier. The most gut-wrenching part was that he didn't recognize us. He was confused and always disoriented. Our lives had changed drastically in such a short time. We were on duty 24/7, standing in front of the doors to prevent him from wandering out into the road. But sometimes he managed to escape. When he wanted to go for a ride, someone had to sit on both sides of him because he would open the door while the car was moving. He used to try to fight everyone, but he never hit me. One day, Krystal stood in front of the back door to keep him from leaving, and he twisted her arm. She burst into tears, and he said, "Shit, I told you to get out of my goddamn way!" After that hit to the head, my Granddaddy was never the same. Exactly six months later, he succumbed to his injuries.

"Wow!" She was in disbelief. Not a word could form in her mouth; she just stared at me. "Girl, I can't imagine going through all of that! Looking at you, you would never know." "You're extremely beautiful, and look at the way you carry yourself. You should be proud! I still have a lot to learn about you, but from what I see, you're amazing," she said.

Our session lasted three hours.

"Hello?" I answered, confused because the caller ID showed

the local police department.

"Is this Ms. Daniels?"

"Yes, this is she."

"Great, how are you? This is Officer Joseph Mack. We have reopened your mom's case. We would like for you and your family to come in for an interview. I will call you back after the holidays." I couldn't believe it! My emotions surged! I didn't know whether to be happy or sad. I was excited that we might finally have closure soon. But on the other hand, my mental health wasn't at its strongest right now, and I knew this could set me back. This wasn't something I could turn my back on, though. If I could help bring justice to my mother's case, I had to. My grandparents died not knowing what happened to their child, and that could easily mean the same for my siblings and me.

Over the past few weeks, I had been under an extreme amount of stress—being misunderstood, battling with my femininity, being everything to the girls but nothing to myself, overthinking, dealing with anxiety, and pushing myself to the max physically, with nowhere to turn. The advice she gave me was enough to get me up to celebrate my birthday.

Feeling relieved, I planned my birthday weekend in Miami. I needed peace. I just wanted to unwind and relax. The day before I was leaving, a guy I'm cool with texted me.

"Be ready by 11; I'm picking you up."

"Okay, I'll see you later," I responded.

"Should I wear sneakers or heels?" I asked before ending the conversation.

"Dress it up; make it look good for me," he replied, followed by a blushing emoji. I laughed.

"Okay, say less!"

Andrea came over to help me get ready. I decided to wear green the whole weekend; it slowly became one of my favorite colors.

Tonight, I started off with a bright green dress with tiny straps, just enough to cover my nipples, revealing my stomach a little lower than my belly button, paired with green strappy heels. Fine as ever!

He and I had been cool for some time now—nothing more. He has multiple businesses, and I've done a lot of business with him. He often called me beautiful and addressed me as "baby." I knew he was a gentleman, so I never took it personally. He'd been to my house on multiple occasions, and we often conversed, but it was strictly for business; he never came inside.

I looked in the mirror, doing my finishing touches, applying my jewelry and makeup. I went to Lona and let her style my hair in soft waves, with lower back-length black curls and a layered side part. I rarely go out because I don't like attention, but when I do, you can believe I'm going to bring it!

"You don't pop your shit enough, friend; you're raw as fuck!" Andrea said excitedly. She always told me that.

As Andrea and I walked outside, he exited a black Range Rover and opened the passenger side door for me. "Please don't make me come find you; this is special cargo," said Andrea. "And don't have her standing up all night either!" We laughed, but she wasn't playing. I knew I was in good hands, though, and he already knew what was up!

When we pulled up at the club, he came around to my side of the car and opened the door for me. He held my hand as we walked to the front. When we entered the club, security directed us to the second floor where our section was. I felt special. Even though I am, people don't just do nice things like that for you if they're not interested in you. And even if they are, they still might not consider you. I felt seen and appreciated by someone who didn't want anything from me at all but to make me feel just the way he did.

I stood up and danced a little in front of him, swaying my hips from side to side while shaking my ass, with him behind me holding my waist.

The bottle girls approached our table, holding bottles and some on ice. I cringed because it drew attention, but I was also thinking, "You did this for me?"

I felt very in tune with my femininity around him because I always knew I was in the presence of a man. But tonight, he made me feel softer—an unusual amount. The way he handled me, I didn't have to say anything.

There were two girls sitting at a table next to us, and one of them couldn't take her eyes off me. He noticed and laughed. "She wants you," he whispered in my ear as we chuckled. She got up and approached me. "You're so beautiful," she said, blushing. She asked what the occasion was. "My birthday!" I yelled over the loud music. "How old did you turn?" she asked. When I told her my age, she couldn't believe it! "Girl, what the fuck, are you serious? You look like a teenager!" I get that all the time, so it wasn't surprising. "Thank you," I said, showing gratitude.

He pulled me closer to him, rubbing my stomach and waist while I caressed his arms and hands. We were both drinking, so saying we were feeling ourselves was an understatement. He ordered so much food for me that the waitresses kept filling our table. I drank until I couldn't handle anymore, and so did he. I know when to stop; I'm lightweight. But he had a little too much.

Temperatures were high, but we didn't let one night lead us astray. He dropped me off at home and waited until I got inside. "I enjoyed you," he texted. "So did I," I responded. After he made it home, we talked briefly until we both fell asleep. The next day, I went to Miami and spent the rest of my time there. I partied every day because I was starting to forget who the hell I was. He texted me the following day, "Where you at, beautiful? I want you with me." But I was so far in Dade and didn't plan on coming home. I loved that I was on his mind, though. We were cool; I never had any intentions of getting with him, but I always admired his hustle and him as a person. He definitely gave off grown man vibes. I was in the dating world; I didn't have anything exclusive going on with anyone, but I was open to possibilities.

After the holidays, Detective Joseph reached out again, and I was delighted to hear from him. He informed me that a body had been found, and a DNA match linked it to the person suspected in my mom's case. He mentioned that the suspect was being transported to their jurisdiction, and they were going to try to get him to confess to each woman he had killed, although that seemed unlikely. As time progressed, he kept in contact, but then, out of nowhere, it stopped. I knew it must have been because he didn't have any news I wanted to hear. With her birthday approaching, I was trying not to dwell on negative thoughts; in fact, I wanted to celebrate it. I was getting back to a better place, especially after my uncle had just died, so I was trying to stay positive.

Surprisingly, a call from Detective Joseph came in.

"Hello, Ms. Daniels. I apologize for not reaching out sooner. This is a really tough case due to the lack of evidence." He began asking me everything I remembered. I started recounting my mom's life as far as I knew. I suggested that we call Kiara, as she could provide him with far more information than I could. We called her, and together we helped him as much as possible. The more he spoke about the different victims' cases involving the same suspect, the more we realized they had failed those women! Evidence was there, and places should have been shut down, but, as we know, money brings power.

Nick was around, but things started to feel draining. He was my only real source of comfort. I mentioned to him when the detective first reached out, but I kept the rest to myself.

The hot-and-cold dynamic intensified the deeper we got. He wasn't running from me; he was running from the person he'd have to become to be with me. I won't lie; it stung because I loved him deeply. The attraction was surface-level, but the connection? That was soul-deep. We both felt it. The energy between us was undeniable—powerful, even. Loving someone like that was an experience that could make you smile or bring you to tears.

When he allowed himself to lean into it, the moments we shared were magical—like the world stood still. But just as I thought we were growing, he'd retreat. And though I sometimes wish I'd never met him, that's not entirely true. I just wish we'd met when he was ready—when growth replaced revenge in his heart, when vulnerability wasn't a fear, and when he'd faced his shadows. I would have stood by him through it all because I'm a healer, and that's what healers do: they trigger growth.

Healing isn't about bringing out the worst; it's about unearthing the best. But that wasn't the journey he was ready for. I longed for the future version of him, the one who would realize the importance of love and connection. What hurt most was knowing he loved me but couldn't show up for me in the way I needed.

I understood it wasn't about me. He had his own battles to face—deep wounds to heal. And I knew I couldn't carry that burden for him. I crave happiness and resolution, not cycles of pain. I refused to let this situation break me in ways I had already healed from.

Being mishandled by people can make you wary, but it hasn't dulled my desire for love. I want affection and a strong, supportive partner—not just for me, but for my daughters. Zuri often talked about wanting a stepdad. When she and I would go out, men often found me attractive, and she would be happy only because she thought it meant a stepdad. I knew then that I had to make different choices. Staying comfortable wasn't an option anymore. Pain can feel familiar, but real growth requires stepping into the unfamiliar.

I've never sought validation, but rejection still leaves its mark. Even when I know someone's actions aren't a reflection of my worth, my mind can play tricks on me. I don't want perfection in a partner—just someone real. Pain is inevitable, but healing can happen through love. Healthy relationships hold you accountable. I want a connection where we can challenge each other to grow.

If you're avoidant, stay and talk. If I'm anxious, give me space to calm down. Let's teach each other what we need. Love can't thrive without communication or compromise. Any person I'm with deserves the best version of me, just as I deserve the best of them.

CHAPTER THIRTEEN

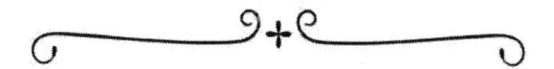

DISCOMPOSED REALITY

The silent treatment from someone you feel deeply connected to can be devastating. It stirs confusion and pain, but I've learned that it often stems from their own fears and unhealed wounds. An intense connection exposes vulnerabilities, and silence becomes a shield. It's rarely about rejection; it's about self-protection.

This journey isn't easy. The cycles of union, separation, and healing teach us to grow, but knowing that doesn't always make it less painful. At times, I've wondered if I was the problem. Why would someone run from the love we shared? But I've realized it's not about me; it's about facing inner shadows and letting go of control.

I felt everything so deeply—the love, the pain, the longing—it consumed me. But silence became my only answer because the rollercoaster was too much. Our bond turned into a battle of pride and pain, and that's not who I am at my core. My love operates from a place of authenticity, not ego.

So, I chose to leave—not out of hate, but because I respected him and myself too much to let things spiral further. Sometimes love means knowing when to let go.

We were becoming so unfamiliar with who we were to one another. We even started to choose disrespectful words, knowing we had never treated each other that way. That was where the line was drawn. That's not what this was, and I refused to carry on that way. A few months ago, he was going through something. He expressed it to me, and it tore me apart, as if I were the one affected. I couldn't eat, I couldn't sleep, and I could barely breathe. I was sick for him! Because of the type of man he was, I understood the depth of his struggle. He didn't even have to express it with such emotion; I still knew. When he came over, I did my best to ease his mind and make him laugh. There were times he told me he was okay and just riding around, but I knew he was crying, given the extent of the situation. He may never know how messed up I was behind it, but Kiara knew I was going through something; I just kept telling her I was okay. I was invested in him. When he came over, things felt much lighter between us. No matter how much he was facing, I could help reverse it, even if just for a moment. But that was then.

Now, most of our words were meant to make one another uncomfortable, mentioning the opposite sex in ways that would bluntly cause frustration. Because of the situation, we grieved silently—sometimes we didn't. After expressing how we were feeling in that moment, too much had been said to take back. Then I would be showered with his vulnerability, my choice of flowers, and my favorite candy. We would make love passionately, but as soon as we parted ways, I was left with a feeling of no longer being relevant. He was mysterious, and without resolution, it was only a matter of time before it resurfaced. The part I played in it was now over.

I understand that people can only offer to the capacity of where they're at, and it's up to you to choose what's best. As much as it hurts, I've come to the realization that Nick isn't what's best for me, and I wasn't what was best for him.

CHAPTER FOURTEEN

SURVIVORS COMPLEX

My inner peace radiated outward, bringing harmony to everyone around me. I was a new woman living a renewed life, wearing my scars like badges of honor and fully embracing everything I had grown into. The life I built for myself was remarkable, especially when I thought about where I started. Watching myself bloom so beautifully was nothing short of inspiring.

I had created a world where whatever I wanted, I could achieve. For Mari and Zuri, there was no waiting or wondering. If they needed or deserved something, it was theirs—no questions asked. My career was thriving, and my hustler mentality kept me moving forward. I didn't know how to sit and wait anymore. I was too driven, too determined, and too much of a mother. Losing everything once taught me that laying down was never an option, even when exhaustion tried to take over.

My expectations for myself were unmatched. Whatever I put

out into the universe manifested because I was intentional, bold, and fearless. My strength wasn't just external; it was my mindset, my resilience, and the way I overcame every obstacle thrown my way. My morals, values, and the way I carried myself set me apart. Nothing could stop me.

I no longer sought validation from anyone. No situation or person intimidated me. For the first time, I truly loved and appreciated myself. I knew exactly what I wanted, and I refused to waver. My confidence was unshakable. I wasn't perfect, but I was comfortable in my skin—my scarred, wounded, beautiful skin.

When people stared, it no longer bothered me. Sometimes it was my injuries that drew their attention, but more often, it was my presence. Strangers would stop me to say how beautiful I was, and I accepted it because I knew it to be true. I showed up for life with purpose every single time, never half-stepping, always fully present. My head was held high, and laughter became my constant companion.

I was proud because I made it. Hurt, alone, broken, in a wheelchair, and undergoing surgery after surgery, I pushed through it all. I'm not fully healed, but I am always healing. My goal is constant improvement—to be better than I was yesterday. I'm grateful I'm not where I used to be, and if this were my final destination, I'd have no regrets.

Happiness began with me. Loving myself set the tone for how others would love me. I've realized that I am enough, and that realization has made all the difference.

I've even accepted that my mom is no longer with us, even without closure. I received another confirmation recently. One of my neighbors called me outside and said she had something to give me. When I walked out, she handed me her card. "I love the woman and mother you are. Take this and spend $100," she said. I was dumbfounded. I couldn't believe it because I didn't know her like that. The more I declined, the more she insisted. After some persuasion, I accepted what she was trying to give me because it reminded me of something Andrea said: "I know you're strong and all, but you have to let someone pour into you as well."

She caught me just before I was pulling away to give me her PIN. After hearing those four numbers, I paused and just stared at her. I felt teary-eyed because I had been struggling mentally like never before, and lately, I had been thinking, "If only I had my mama!" Her PIN was literally my mom's birthday. In that moment, I felt complete. She was still looking out for me, sending angels to complete the mission she couldn't.

Healing is all about removing the limitations you place upon yourself. If you put them there, you can take them away. It's about deciding to let go of everything that once held you down and becoming free. I had a way of seeing people's true intentions. I was so aware of it that it was also saddening. The discernment would come to me quickly, causing me to adjust. To some, I seemed mean. Kiara once told me, "All those men like you and try to talk to you, but you end up turning them away just to be alone. You have to let that guard down and let somebody love you. You deserve that. You're so beautiful, Maj; these girls need a dad too."

But people only knew what I showed them, what I allowed them to see. I'd been in the dating world for a while now, and there were a few times I gave people a fair chance to court me—more than enough, actually. I'm a lover. No matter what, I will forever choose love, and Kiara knew that. I guess my tough exterior blinded it a little. Because I loved softly and healthily, I was careful about who I gave it to. Not everyone was deserving. I could give a guy the chance he begged for, and he still wouldn't know what to do with it. They don't keep their word, no dates, no leadership, but expect you to let them stick around. We're too grown for this. What are we doing? How will this benefit either of us? How will I ever be comfortable enough to bask in my femininity if I'm the one leading?

Also, because of my forgiving heart, it's easy to find yourself accepting all kinds of nonsense. That's why Kiara never saw things get far after I started dating someone. Once I saw inconsistencies or disrespect—whether towards me or another woman—it was over. Once I see you don't carry yourself as a grown man should, I don't want anything else to do with you. It's not always easy. There are times I've been hurt, and not only because of Nick.

There were moments I had to catch it early because, as women, we tend to hold on to a little potential we see. I can't get stuck like that. I've never been abused or truly disrespected by a man I was dealing with, and I'd like to keep it that way. Steve was as bad as it ever got. Things weren't all good, but I learned what not to accept ever again after him.

I don't play with men at all! And that was my superpower. I wasn't just out here having casual sex, so I was able to walk in my power at all times. Sex was healing; the exchange of energy from someone pouring back into you was one of the highest vibrations to manifest. That's what sex was to me—tantric.

So if a real one ever presented himself to me, trust me, I know what to do with him.

The night Kiara met Ty, before our date, he had her sold. Being chocolate and fine didn't help either. There wasn't much to doubt then, but not long after, it became clear he wanted to waste my time. I often heard, "You make me nervous. You really like that? You don't find women like you? What are you hiding?" It sounded like I was just too good to be true—once again.

Sometimes I get caught up trying to figure out how someone can be that good if it never works out. I speak to myself.

But this guy once told me, "Most men want what comes easy. They say they want something good, but they're not willing to put in the effort it takes to earn it. The truth is, a lot of women out here make it easy, so that's who they choose. But there are some men who appreciate a challenge, and those are the ones worth waiting for—because they won't be easily swayed or distracted." He said they aren't ready for that kind of pressure. "You're confident, you talk that talk, you're smart, you've got your life together, and they see that. It's not you; it's them!"

It was time to go back into the OR. Dr. Jessie was doing something similar to what he had done in the first surgery. I needed another flap, taking muscle from the right side of my stomach and adding it to another part of my left thigh that needed to be filled. More surgeries meant more scars. To be honest, they never really phased me, but the more I went through, the more extravagant they became. This time, I felt a little disturbed. The procedures were more severe this time. Flap surgeries were kind of like an extension cord; they had to run from the source down to the supplier. So it started on the right side of my stomach, going down to above my pubic area, turning left, and going down that leg to supply the thigh, leaving a cut in the crease of my thigh next to my vagina. I had no idea it would be this intense.

The pain was unbearable. I kept feeling swelling and an immense amount of pain in my vagina, but I didn't know what was going on. I thought it was coming from my stomach. I couldn't see my stomach because I had on an ace bandage. When I got home, I was scared to use the bathroom because I knew my anxiety would make me feel uneasy in my stomach. Sure enough, when I pulled down my pants, I almost passed out. It was very swollen, and it scared the hell out of me! I thought it was going to stay that way.

I held back tears as I shut myself in the bathroom because Andrea and Kiara were in my room. When I walked out, I acted like everything was fine. But depression had just set in. I didn't say anything to them because I didn't want them to make me feel worse once they saw it.

The Easter holiday was a few days away, and I was in distress, but I had to get up. The girls were putting a lot of pressure on me. As bad as I wanted to continue lying there, I couldn't. I took them for their baskets, and we went out to eat. Sitting at the table, I was in so much pain that all I could do was burst into tears. I couldn't even walk. I could barely sit down. But being at home was even more detrimental to me right now.

I couldn't keep neglecting myself like this. I couldn't keep thinking that the more I could handle, the stronger I was. And why did I need to be so strong anyway? Even if no one was coming to save me and I had to save myself, why couldn't I do it softly? No one talks about going through something so traumatic and then living through it. Because now you have a constant fear of being weak. They say trauma makes you stronger, but it doesn't. It gave me depression, anxiety, trust issues; it broke me and gave me sleepless nights. But it made me feel like I had to be strong because I survived something so irregular. I looked at myself as superwoman now, and I just wanted to put that down.

My femininity was right there but seemed so hard to grasp. I feel it all inside of me. It filled my aura. My aesthetic was just that.

I was a girl's girl, and I greeted everyone with a smile. I was loving and soft. But somehow, I was also hard as nails. In the blink of an eye, I had to become the mom yelling after saying something so many times that it never got done. I was fighting with my teenager, who thought she was grown now and wanted to taste the world. I was defending myself to a guy who never had the intention of hearing me anyway.

And there it was—it hit me! I had to let it all go! I had been the best mother I knew how to be. If I didn't provide it—whether emotionally, physically, or financially—it was because I couldn't. I didn't have it to give. I gave to those girls until I felt depleted; no one could ever play with me as a mother in this lifetime or the next! I spoiled them so much that now Mari felt entitled. She was selfish and inconsiderate. I hated her personality! She was a downer, never happy unless it benefited her. And because I struggled with my mental health, I usually did what I thought needed to be done to fix the situation. So now I had a child who sometimes felt undeserving, thinking there were no rules. But this was where I had to make the shift because she really had me messed up.

Anytime Steve would lie to her, saying he was going to do something and didn't, she would become upset and start acting out. It happened every time. She even stopped performing well in school. I'm very involved and stay on top of the things they want for their future. But her mind wasn't on school anymore or doing what was right. I have this mother wound in me so big that I try to heal through my girls. I go above and beyond to make sure I'm filling every void. I usually perform well, but there will always be this one space I can't fill, and that's being her dad.

He makes her feel worthless; I constantly have to speak life into her. He makes her cry, and I have to dry those tears. But she loves him to the end of the earth, accepting the little crumbs he decides to sprinkle on her every now and then. That's what she has decided to accept from boys as well now. I always tell her, "Good girls finish last! Don't worry about what the other girls are doing. Don't worry about why that boy isn't interested in you. Just stay presentable. Keep your character and aura intact, so when it's time for those things, they won't pass you by. It may take a little longer because you're a good girl doing it the right way. But you'll be able to obtain it because of the way you did it." Nick was my confidant, and I couldn't even talk to him about it. He often told me I couldn't keep things like this from him, but I felt like the world was against me. This time, there wasn't a reason to, because they both had already killed me softly.

Andrea often told me our children are here to show us what we need to heal in ourselves. Because Mari was very selfish, I needed to start being that way with myself. She assured me that I was too freely giving and often neglected myself. I then noticed that Zuri was too emotional and realized that was also something I had to heal in myself because I wasn't affectionate.

I saw my child fading away right in front of me, and I've done all I can to save her. But I had to keep going; I still have Zuri, who deserves the world. She's innocent to so many things. I can still save her. Having to give up on your child and let them learn for themselves is an awful feeling. Only the Lord knows. But for my sanity, I have to let go.

That means letting go of a man whose energy was unsure of me. Someone my girls love to death, but it's still not enough. If it meant my daughters getting misconstrued on what love is or what I chose to accept, I had to let it go. They wanted a dad so badly that I felt sorry for them. In a way, I played a role in it as well; I had a man calling himself their stepdad, but he could only show up moderately. He helped out with what they needed but was still right in their face saying "NO." All of this was causing my defenses to go up. Even us talking about babies and going on more dates, just to pull away—knowing he loved me but was depriving me of it.

Nothing soft was coming out of these situations until I chose to address the problems and then adjust.

My counseling sessions were helping. She gave me tough tasks to confront but showed my vulnerability. Things that made me say, "Hell no, I ain't doing that!" made me feel weak, like I was begging a man. But I would be proud of myself after I did it because of how much courage it took, even if the outcome broke my heart.

When you choose to stop communicating, you're also shifting your relationship with yourself. You're reclaiming your time, your energy, and your sense of identity. You're reminding yourself that your worth isn't tied to someone else's approval. The moment you stop chasing and stand still, you create space for the right things to find their way to you.

I was losing two of the people I loved most in this lifetime, and I wasn't okay. Rico was my heart and was usually there for me at these times, but he's done something so unforgivable that I've lost him as well. I'm grieving three people who are still alive, and I'm suffering. But I had to do this for me. If I wanted to save myself, the little of what I had left, if I wanted to become the softest, happiest version of myself, I had to.

I'm sure Mari will eventually understand. But Nick, this was the end for us. I feel it in my soul. I still love him like no one I've ever encountered, and I still respect him to the utmost, but we are done.

Rico used to ask me, "What does it feel like, Auntie, to have a relationship like you and Nick? I've never seen anyone love each other like you two." I could never give him an answer because I didn't want to think about it.

But if I had to answer now, I'd say, "A divine counterpart feels like a near-death experience. You get into a car accident, go into a black tunnel, see the light, reach the light, and meet God. You feel and understand things that you could not feel and understand before. You experience one hundred percent of something that cannot be compared to earthly soulmate love. It feels as if you are not only standing in the sun and feeling its rays; you are the sun. You are one hundred percent in a God-like state. There are no thoughts, doubts, fears, or 'what ifs'—just pure love and only pure love. There are no words that can describe the purity of that kind of love.

Then something calls you back. You don't want to go back, but you do. You see yourself from above: your life, your behavioral patterns, your flawed programming, and the world as one, yet all that separation from the source remains. However, you are sent back. You wake up in a hospital bed, unable to believe what you just experienced. The biggest shock is that you see your life, the world, and humanity in a different light. Everything is different because your perception of reality has changed 360 degrees since your experience with the source.

You want to go back, but you cannot. You didn't just meet the source; you have become the source. Or rather, you are now aware of the source within you. You see all these people on the streets passing by, "unawakened," and you almost feel like an alien. You feel lonelier than ever before in your life, yet at the same time, you are more whole than ever. You become an entity—calm and at eternal peace.

That, in short, is what a divine counterpart encounter does within you. The same happens to him, maybe shortly before or shortly after you met. All this occurs separately.

Meanwhile, life around you goes on as if nothing happened, but everything has changed. The encounter with your divine counterpart has turned both of your lives upside down—fears, commitments, real 3D issues, running, chasing, distance, logic, and ego all play a role. Values and responsibilities also come into play. After a true divine encounter, usually neither party is looking for love anymore. It's like searching for God after you've already found Him. So you keep God deep in your heart and move on with your life.

That's what it's like. And people knew. My family loved him. Kiara and Krystal admired him. I knew he loved me, but his way of expressing that love was detrimental to me.

I'll never be naive enough to think another woman didn't play a role in his life that affected our relationship; it's just that I couldn't be bothered on any level. No matter who she was or what she had, that has always been the least of my concerns because I created my own lane, and there was no getting over it. I didn't desire to be like anyone else or obtain what they had. I was that girl!

My scars healed and looked better, but my body was literally reconstructed. Over fifty percent was scarred. I have more upcoming surgeries, and I'm not sure when it will end. It took an extreme amount of confidence to embrace this journey. Each time I went to Dr. Jessie's office, they showered me with love because of my ability to show so much gratitude. Going in there lighthearted and positive, I knew I was fortunate. I didn't go through this experience to stay the same. I encountered something extraordinary, and I held onto that light.

I am exclusively dating. Eventually, I'll get my happy ending the right way. Because I, too, know that "good girls finish last!"

Also Available On Amazon